SOCIAL STATUS MATTERS

Ahmed Riahi-Belkaoui

ISBN: 1-4392-6267-5
EAN13: 9781439262672

TO HEDI

"Aux ames bien nees, la valeur n'attends pas le nombre des annees"

LIST OF TOPICS

INTRODUCTION

Social status is as important to our daily life as oxygen. It was adequately compared to a man's alimentary canal. "Social status in America is somewhat like man's alimentary canal; he may not like the way it works and he may want to forget that certain parts of it are part of him, but he knows it is necessary for his very existence. A status system, often an object of our disapproval, is present and necessary in our complex social world."[1]

Whether implicit or overt, classification by social status is a human universal. It defines us in terms of our relative access to resources, determines our behavior and attitudes, and influences our social and market interactions. It is derived from the Latin term, ***Standische Lage***,for "**standing**" which indicates one's position in society.

Status hierarchies are agreements, maintained by **deference signals**, to facilitate social and market interactions. We are hard-wired to rank every aspect of our lives. For every characteristic that shapes our lives, our environment, and our own thinking, there is a rating that indicates our rank, and thereby, our status level on a given characteristic. The process results in our assignment to a high-, middle- or low-status level, leading us to a **weltanschauung** or view-of -the world, that comes with benefits and costs to which we must to react or adapt. The consequences range from the good to the bad to the ugly, making social status the ultimate object of desire.

This book intends to explicate the concept of social status, its antecedents, and its consequences as presented in the social sciences literature and research.The reader should benefit from the results of the research and learn to adjust his (or her life) to the merits and impact of social status. The reader will be left with one recurring thought about social status: Never leave home without it.

I would like to thank both Professors Malcolm McLelland and Ronald Picur for a very thoughtful and helpful review of the book. **Social status matters and friendship matters more.**

1. WHAT IS SOCIAL STATUS?

The concept of social status was first introduced by Max Weber as an "effective claim to social esteem in terms of negative or positive privileges".[2] It is a **socially-constructed** asset, position, or rank that yields (or limits) access to resources. The focus is on position or rank in relation to others. One's status is always relative to that of someone else. It is relevantly defined as "a ranking in a hierarchy that is socially recognized and typically carries with it the expectation of entitlement to certain resources."[3]

A social system consists of well-defined **social roles** associated with varying levels of prestige, responsibility, and power. Roles may be defined as "the bundles of socially-defined attributes and expectations associated with social positions."[4] These roles serve as status signals that define the social rank of the person assigned that role and the traits required to attain it. For example, being assigned the role of a manager confers a specific status on an employee relative to employees in other relevant roles.

The desire for status operates through emotions and inborn tastes. As stated by Frank: "feelings and emotions, apparently, are the proximate causes of most behaviors...Rational calculations are an input into the [internal] reward mechanism."[5]

Status is pursued as a reward. A revealing example of the pursuit of status as an end in scientific circles is evident in the well-known mathematicians' toast: "To pure mathematics-and may it never be of any use to anybody!"[6] The crucial feature is that "social status rests on collective judgment, or rather a consensus of opinion within a group. No one person can by himself confers status on another, and if a man's position were assessed differently by everybody he met, he would have no status at all."[7]

Hobbes wrote that men are continuously in competition for honor and dignity.[8] One can easily assume that many people would pay large sums of money for knighthood or the Nobel Prize. What they seek are social status and social rewards, important motivations for behavior and deference by others.

Status may be viewed as a non-coerced, interindividual, within-group form of social asymmetry, resulting from an accumulation of acknowledgment and reverence. Classifications of status abound. One classification views status as either **"legal"**, **"traditional"**, and **"charismatic"**.[9] Another classification views status as **"ascribed"**, or **"achieved."** It is also viewed as either a **hierarchy of rewards** or a **hierarchy of displays**. The rewards hierarchy implies a hierarchy of privilege with those of high status having access to desirable things and a relatively stable acquiescence (begrudging or not) from the "have-nots".[10] The acceptance of the **"have-nots"** is generally due to the fact that status arises most often from nonagonistic sources such as excellence in valued domains of activity.[11] Those who acquired status from excellence in valued domains are said to have "**prestige**".

Status may be ascribed in the sense that it has been assigned, or achieved in the sense that has been acquired on the basis of merit. Factors determining ascribed status include age, kinship, sex, race, group, caste, citizenship, and religion. Achieved status reflects personal skills, abilities and efforts. Education, occupation, and marital status contribute to the achieved status assignment.

Both achieved and ascribed status can be used by an individual to choose a **master status** or social position to be considered as the primary identifying characteristic of an individual. In fact, observers often base their assessments of an individual's status in whole or in part, on observable qualities of the individuals, referred to as status characteristics. A **status characteristic** has been defined as " a characteristic of an actor that has two or more states that are differentially evaluated in terms of honor, esteem, or desirability, each of which is associated with distinct moral and performance expectations, that is, with beliefs about how an individual possessing a given state of the characteristic will perform or behave."[12] It implies that a status characteristic affects people's expectations of the performance capabilities of those persons who possess the valued characteristic.

A group's hierarchy of power and prestige is created as a result of these expectations, leading individuals of low-status to defer to or be influenced by those of high-status;these status characteristics can be specific or general. Specific status characteristics pertain to those affecting specific knowledge and/or specific situations. General status characteristics are not restricted. Examples of general characteristics include age, gender, race, beauty, height, educational abilities, et cetera. Research shows that any characteristic that allows a differentiation among subjects can become a status characteristic, affecting a participant's influence within the group and their claim to the common resources of the group.[13] Status characteristics theory seeks to describe **status-consciousness**, the idea that if members of a group can be differentiated by some valued characteristic, they will form expectations of the performance capabilities of each other based on this characteristic. It is even argued that status characteristics, like education level and formal rank, not only generate expectations of competence but also give higher status actors an influence in task-oriented interactions.[14] This may explain why it was found that junior college students were more influenced by a partner they believe came from a private university than a partner they believe was from a high school,[15] and higher ranked military personnel were more influential than lower ranked privates when interacting to solve a novel and non-military task.[16]

Under cultural sociology the status distinction is maintained by cultural exclusiveness, with two related versions of status, **status as lifestyle** (cultural status) and **status as political-legal entitlement** (the citizenship component of status). Status as lifestyle is nothing more than the set of cultural practices and rituals or **"habitus"**_ in terms of the dress, speech, taste and view of the world making up the individuals' perceptions of the social world.[17]

2. WHAT DO YOU WANT: SOCIAL STATUS, SOCIOECONOMIC STATUS, POPULARITY, LEADERSHIP OR POWER?

You may be tempted to answer that you want it all. It is possible but highly unlikely to possess all these qualities. It is important to understand the differences between these desirable qualities before making a choice or settling for one or more of them.

Social status within face-to-face groups is very contextual and best defined in reference to a particular group. It is best characterized as involving the acquisition and bundling of **prominence, respect**, and **influence.**[18]

First, social status implies *prominence* in the sense that those higher in the hierarchy receive more attention than those lower in the hierarchy.[19] The end result is that the individual designed to have social status will be the center of attention leaving everybody else to play the role of followers.

Second, social status implies *respect* in the sense that the higher status members are shown more respect and held in higher regard than the lower status members.[20] So, a welcoming deference protocol and behaviors shown to higher social status members may be lacking for lower status members.

Third, social status implies *influence* in the sense that the higher status members are allowed more authority over group decisions and processes.[21] What ever they say on the issues under consideration is taken into account and possibly acted upon.

It is this contextual nature of prominence, respect, and influence that differentiates *social status* from other related concepts involving social functioning and success, such as *socioeconomic status, popularity, leadership* and *power*.

Socioeconomic status (or SES) is generally used to refer to an economic and sociological measure of an individual, as defined in terms of income, education, occupation and wealth. It is generally broken into three categories, high SES, middle SES, and low SES. So, one may conceive of a high SES individual with low social status, and easily visualize a low SES individual, such as a priest or a professor with high social status. Being successful in the chosen occupation as well as education and wages contribute to SES in contrast to social status which is established by peer ratings.

Popularity is the quality of being well-liked or even common. Popularity calls for respect of the popular person given by peers, as well as respect shown by the popular person to peers. It also calls for amicability in the sense that a popular person shows how much he/she likes others, since a person who does not like others is unlikely to be liked by others. One may easily conceive of a popular person lacking social status and vice versa. Popular persons are known for their warmth, love, nurturance, altruism, and communion, all related to the broader five dimensions of **Agreeableness.**[22] Because social status represents a bundling of SES, popularity (hence agreeableness), and leadership, however, a person of high status does not necessarily need to be agreeable to gain prominence, respect and influence.

Leadership implies the social influence fitness needed to convince people to work for the accomplishment of a common task that will be beneficial to group welfare. Unlike social status, leadership calls for devising a management strategy that will lead to accomplishment of the common task. While in most cases leaders may have prominence and influence, they don't necessary always have the respect of others.[23] There is also the general perception that in most cases leaders are muddling through and claim wisdom when things go right- a clear case of **fooled by randomness**. Add to that the myth that the leader is like an orchestra conductor. Witness the following comment:

> "It's this idea of standing on a pedestal and you wave your baton and accounting comes in, and you wave it somewhere else and marketing chimes in with accounting, and they all sound very glorious. But management is more like orchestra conducting during rehearsals, when everything is going wrong"[24]

So, an effective leader is more of a composer than a conductor and leadership effectiveness is best achieved when the leader has also high social status.

Status is also different from **power**. While social status implies a rank ordering of individuals or groups on the basis of respect and prestige accorded by audiences of interest, power implies a rank ordering on the basis of control of resources. Power may be viewed in one of two ways. In **power-dependency theory**, power implies dependence, whereby the power of actor A over actor B has a value equivalent to the dependence of B on A.[25] In **elementary theory**, power is equivalent to the structural capacity to extract valued resources.[26] With social status, there is a relative state of respect between the parties, while with power there is a relative state of control and dependence. The low-power party depends on the high-power party for access or assignment to positively valued resources such as rewards, or to negatively valued resources such as punishments. It was even argued that power has metamorphic consequences, with a tendency of those with high power to roam in a very different psychological space than those with low power.[27] For example, women who were involved in directing their housekeepers devalued the abilities of the housekeepers more than women who were less involved, due to their own sense of control over the capacity of the housekeepers to complete their work effectively.[28]

Power, with its ability to generate compliance, obedience, and conformity, and to set agendas and rules of conduct, relies on control and dominance. In contrast, social status may be able to achieve the same results in an atmosphere of respect.Power may come with status or without status. Where it comes without status, power is just coercion, intimidation, punishment-centered, involuntary, or imposed with people complying with the wishes of the person holding power in order to avoid potential punishment. Where power comes with status, it is a power where influence is legitimate, voluntary or endorsed, and where people believe the person holding the power has status and deserves it. It is important to note that there are cases where status comes without power. It was argued that "in some societies high prestige status is sometimes possessed by learned or holy men whose economic and political status are both low [and that] there are many examples of dispossessed aristocracies, which maintained a high prestige status for some time after losing both their money and power."[29]

The discussion here suggests it is more practical and satisfying to seek a position of leadership and popularity that is associated with a high status level than a similar position relying on the exercise of power and the signaling of high SES.

3. IS THE HUMAN BRAIN "HARD WIRED" FOR STATUS?

It is interesting to find out what makes us happier: cash or social status. Two experiments offered useful insights in how the brain is processing social and economic rewards.

In the first study, the researchers presented evidence showing that money and praise go hand in hand.[30] Basically, making money and getting a positive reputation engaged much of the same reward circuitry. The brain's reward system, called **the striatum**, works similarly for both praise and money. In other words, a social reward is processed in the striatum in the same way a monetary reward is processed. This finding is in support of the civilized behavior of offering genuine compliments as rewards since it seems to activate the same reward center in the brain as paying cash rewards. It also validates the long-held assumption that people get a psychological boost from a good reputation. Social reward is *biologically coded,* indicating that the need to belong is essential to humans.

In the second study, the researchers explored the neural regions activated when people process information on their social status.[31] They saw increased activity in the brain reward center when people either won money or saw their social standing rise. The key findings follow:

1. Social status is highly valued, as suggested by the finding that the ventral striatum-the area that signals an event's importance- reacted to changes either a rise or fall in rank as much as it reacted to monetary award.

2. Just viewing an individual ranked as "superior" activated an area at the front of the brain that appears to specialize in sizing others up and assessing social status.

3. Different brain areas are activated when a person moves up or down on a pecking order, or simply views perceived social superiors or inferiors. Performing better than a superior activated areas higher and toward the front of the brain, while performing worse than an inferior activated areas lower in the brain associated with emotional pain and frustration. In other words, an impending upgrade in status produced similar changes to winning money in the brain's "value center". A downgrade in status activated circuitry known to process emotional pain and frustration.

4. People who felt more joy when they won also felt more pain when they lost.

The finding suggests gaining social status makes us as happy as getting monetary rewards. It is really status, and not cash, which is king. The findings argue positively for the civilized behavior of giving compliments and social awards when warranted. They provide a clear support for the thesis that the brain is "hard wired" to recognize, assess, and receive status.

So humans are wired to rank the best. Once, survival was at stake. Witness the following observation made in a New York Times article: "caring about who is best comes from a function that originally has to do with survival...You would want the person who represented you to be the best at it-because without them being the best, or winning, you might starve to death or be attacked. That part is neurologically set in. We are ranking and ordered animals."[32]

In conclusion, it is much wiser to give a better place to social awards and status upgrades when recognizing someone's positive contribution since a wider range of social awards and status upgrades can be provided to reward the contribution. So, status-not cash- is the real king and has a special place in the brain.

4. WHAT COMES WITH SOCIAL STATUS? (DON'T LEAVE HOME WITHOUT IT.)

If you happen to reach a high social status, this is what you should expect:

1. High social status is associated with greater benefits than low social status in many contexts, such as:

- -better physical and mental health,[33]
- -better pay, [34]
- -greater decision authority and "airtime" in workgroups,[35] and,
- -better value and respect by others than low status individuals.[36]

2. On average, high status individuals are stereotyped as more **"self-concerned"**, and less **"other-concerned"** than low status individuals. They are seen as more ambitious, confident, and dominant than low status individuals, but also less warm, sincere, and good-natured. This relationship between social status and social motive stereotypes was confirmed for different social categories (e.g. rich people, Asians, housewife, and elderly people), [37]and occupations (e.g. stockbroker, surgeon, legal clerk, and telephone operators).[38]

3. High status individuals are often assumed by society to have experience and expertise in a wide variety of domains, even when there is no specific evidence suggesting that they possess skills in a particular area.[39]

4. High status individuals may also be stereotyped as more intelligent and competent than low status individuals.[40] With the high expectations of competence assigned to high status individuals, such individuals find themselves with more opportunities and rewards, given that high status represents also a "taken for granted" association between rewards and performance outcomes.[41]

5. The higher your status is, the harder you may fall: Observers attribute greater intentionality to the actions of high status wrongdoers than they attribute to identical actions of low status wrongdoers; and, consequently recommends more severe punishments for the former than the latter.[42] This is mainly driven by observers' perceptions of the wrongdoer's underlying social motives: High status wrongdoers are presumed to be more interested in their own welfare (self-concerned), and less interested in the welfare of others (other-concerned), than low status individuals.[43] This is a good example of a situation where social status is more of a liability than an asset.

6. There is definitively a positive stereotyping bias towards high status persons. The evidence shows that people hold trait-like stereotypes about those in high- and low- status positions; believing, for example, that the former are more competent, intelligent, and even better looking than the latter.[44] [45] [46] High status individuals are judged with more leniency than lower status individuals, who are evaluated with stricter standards.[47]

7. Status is also linked to power. Power implies control over others' incomes[48], implying the ability to influence others' behavior.[49] People with power are often attributed higher status.[50] With regards to status, at a psychological level, greater **prestige** implies **referent power**. High status individuals are admired and may be emulated.[51] Status leads to exert power, as high status individuals are assumed to be more competent. Status also allows for greater reward and punishment power, since recognition by high status individuals is likely to be more valuable to others.[52]

8. High status produces tangible benefits where high status people conceded higher benefits by their lower status counterparts in negotiation,[53] and market interchanges,[54] due to people with lower status being willing to adopt beliefs that disfavor themselves versus their higher status counterparts.[55]

9. Workers with status concerns will have more high-powered incentives, work more, and earn more than workers who do not care about status.[56]

10. When it comes to social comparisons, higher social status is more beneficial, since social comparisons are more satisfying to the individual when they imply a superior position for the focal individual. In fact, working with similar-status others allows individuals to positively compare themselves to different others and derive positive self-identity resources based on their status.[57] It follows that

a) similarity among high-status individuals leads to stronger in-group favoritism than similarity of low-status individuals,[58] and b) an individual of any status finds membership in a high-status in-group more attractive than membership in a low-status group.[59]

10. When working with high-status individuals, a low-status individual may learn and acquire behavior associated with higher performance.[60] For example, it was shown that low-status school children performed better when they worked together with high-status students on an independent task than when they worked with similar low-status students.[61]

11. Social status may lead to a drive towards **social fitness** since potential members who care about status are likely to engage in activities and interactions that produce higher fitness, and to be even willing to pay for status.

12. Status is consistently valued across settings, with higher status consistently affording advantages in social interaction. There are however two possibilities.

According to a **status attainment perspective**, the higher one's status, regardless of the status of his or her immediate coworkers, the better it is for the individual in the organization. Status is value laden so that higher status provides advantages within an organization while low status can have negative implications.[62]

According to a **status disparity perspective**, being similar to others regardless of status level may be more advantageous than being high in status. A difference between an individual's status level and those of coworkers ("status disparity") may have negative effects on the experience of the focal individual.[63]

13. Conferring status on a group of individuals legitimizes their natural sense of superiority and makes them feel that they deserve, and thus should work to obtain, better outcomes for members of their own group.[64] This is especially true when status emerges directly out of competitive conflict: "...every individual finds himself in a struggle for status; a struggle to preserve his personal prestige, his point of view, and his self-respect. He is able to maintain them, however, only to the extent that he can gain for himself the recognition of everyone else whose estimate seems important."[65]

14. Resources can acquire status value which causes their rate of exchange to change. For example, it was reported that actor Don Johnson placed his 1970 yellow Barracuda up for sale at the Jackson Classic car Auction in Scottsdale, Arizona.[66] "Come on, everybody, my butt was on that seat," pleaded the actor prior to the bidding. His plea worked as the car sold for $148,500; more than ten times the 'coda' book value. So, the status value spread from the person to the exchangeable resource. Obviously, resources held by higher status actors are perceived to have greater status value than resources held by lower status actors. This is known as the **status value**

theory as status characteristics produce power and the possession of valued resources allows power to be exercised by high-status actors.

5. WHAT COMES WITH STATUS DEFERENCE?

An individual's status is the "degree of **deference**, esteem and power to influence others" he or she acquires.[67] Stated differently, status emerges from a flow of deference. When a person engages in a status deference behavior, the person is making ordinal rank distinctions between actors in a power and prestige ordering. Closeness to, or distance from, social centers of power, values, norms and legitimacy indicates the deference-entitling characteristics.

The most commonly cited indicators of proximity to social centers and which are liable to generate status deference are:

1. occupational position,
2. educational attainment,
3. race,
4. gender,
5. ethnicity,
6. religion, and even,
7. height.[68]

Status deference arises from the linkages between individuals, their statuses, and their concomitant rights and duties, leading to the view of status as a **"deference-position".**[69] The use of verbal and non-verbal status behaviors to signal their subordinate or super ordinate status rank can be either appreciative or derogative. Appreciating one's position assessment of another is recognition of high deference. A derogative or negative assessment of another is recognition of low deference. It is a way of highlighting the power and prestige differences between individuals.

The following situations arise as a result of status deference:[70]

1. **Reciprocal acts of deference** or **mutual deference** are a way of signaling symmetry in the status rank that interacting individuals have achieved in the hierarchy of outside society.[71]

2. **Symmetrical acts of deference** are a way of signaling actors' shared ordinal position when compared to the rank of others in a given hierarchy system.

3. The **verbal and non-verbal status behaviors** calling for deference may be viewed as culturally-meaningful indicators of social rank.[72]

4. Promoting **mutually desirable outcomes**, often requires lower status actors to yield to higher status actors through status deference.[73]

5. **Culturally prescribed roles** dictating respective entitlements and obligations also calls for status deference.

6. People tend to tolerate the physical nearness of high-status people and to distance themselves from low-status people.[74] Such difference in behavior may explain why people assist high-status individuals more readily than they assist low-status individuals.[75] It also explains why some pedestrians were more likely not to obey crosswalk signals when following the example of an offender of obvious high status (e.g. wearing a suit, a tie, and a hat) than when following that of an offender of

obviously lower status (e.g. wearing dirty, heavy cotton trousers, and a faded tee shirt).[76]

While most cases of status deference assume an uncontested context, there are various cases where status is literally **"taken"**, such in elementary school playgrounds,[77] street gangs,[78] academic seminars, and meeting among executives.[79]

6. DO HIGH STATUS INDIVIDUALS ASK AND GET COMPLIANCE FROM OTHERS?

People need each other's help and support in various situations daily. Nobody can truly navigate a complex modern life without getting the appropriate assistance. What is required is to ask and hope for assistance or compliance especially in those cases where those complying have never been rewarded or do not expect to receive a monetary or non-monetary reward. Because people differ in terms of social status conditions, one would expect different scenarios when the person doing the "asking" has higher status than the one doing the "complying". This results from the thesis that schemas of social categories often influence the impression a person has of others.[80] As a result, the schemas about members of these social categories will likely affect judgments, behavior, expectations and evaluations of a person who belongs to one of those categories.[81] In other words, once a person has been judged as fitting a particular category, schemas about members of that group may affect expectations, influences, and judgment about that person. To date, the evidence indicates that individuals with a high social status have a positive impact on compliance when they solicit help from people of lower social status. More precisely:

1.People were found to be more readily willing to give a coin to a stranger in the street if the individual is neatly dressed rather than to someone whose appearance was untidy.[82] The same result was found when the solicitation was aimed at raising money for a charitable organization.[83] The "high status"- like appearance motivated and provided an implicit rationale for the giving.

2. People were found to be more willing to give back money they found in a telephone booth to a high status individual when this person made a case that the money was his or hers, than if it was an individual of equal status making the case for the money.[84] Higher status people are expected to be more believable and more honest than lower status people.

3. Pro-social behavior involves deliberate responses to assist, collaborate, share, give care, take turn, or be friendly, kind, and show compassion, and sympathy. Status has an impact on prosocial behavior. People were found to be more willing to help a high status woman than a mid-status woman who had dropped her groceries while loading the trunk of her car.[85] The finding suggests helping a lower status person will cause the individual providing the help to lose status, while helping a higher status person may "rub off" and give the helper an upgrade in status.

These results point to a situation where high status individuals are more likely to be:

a) on the receiving end of a contribution,

b) considered to be believable and honest, and

c) on the receiving end of help.

It appears that high status people have just to ask and they receive help and compliance from others. In fact, once high-status is established it becomes an asset for its holder,[86] who is often given more credit than is a low-status individual for the same amount of effort. Basically, following an increase in the status of an individual, there is also an increase in the propensity of others to over-estimate the quality of his or her performance, an increase in the individual's success relative to other individuals in the market, and even the likelihood of being chosen as preferred exchange partner.[87]

7. HOW DO WE THINK ABOUT SOCIAL STATUS?

It is important in our daily social life to be able to recognize one's own status and the status of others in the group. Given knowledge of one's status, one is bound and is expected to adopt a proper role in interacting with others.[88] High status individuals not only have preferential access to resources, they also know how to elicit the appropriate behavior from those of lower rank. High-status individuals typically spend a longer time speaking relative to listening in a social conversation relative to low-status individuals, a phenomenon known as the **"visual dominance ratio"**.[89] At the same time, those at a lower rank expect to be protected and taken care of by people of higher rank.[90]

The question is whether we are able to have a mental representation of the ranking that underlies the assignment of status to individuals in a group. The answer is positive in the case on non-human primates who seem to have the ability to store and retrieve knowledge about their own and others' rank in the social hierarchy.[91] In the case of humans, it is plausible that the human ability to successfully navigate hierarchical social interaction arises from adaptive mechanisms in the mind[92] and brain[93] for recognizing social status signals from complex sensory input.

Evidence suggesting the existence of cognitive mechanisms that allow mental representations of knowledge about non-social domains ranges from the abstract such as numbers and letters in the alphabet,[94] to the perceptual such as hue and size.[95] In the case of numbers, there is a **"distance effect"** where the amount of time it takes to compare two numbers is an inverse function of how much numerical distance separates those numbers.[96] For example, it is faster to compare 5 to 100 than it is to compare 5 to 6. The distance effect is also present in the cases of letters in the alphabet and the relative size of objects.

Do humans have the same mental representations than non-human primates when it comes to social status? An experiment investigated the nature of social status and numbers of representations using a semantic distance latency test.[97] The results show that participants were fastest when comparing large differences in status ranks and also have mental representations of social status that share properties with such diffeerences. The authors conclude as follows:

> "Our results indicate that knowledge of social status is an abstract domain, like number, in that symbolic cues mediate the processing of status perception from perceptual cues (such as occupational labels and visual insignias) to an amodal, internal representation of its semantic meaning. Although both domains are organized in a similar analogical fashion, status is a domain distinguished from number, perhaps resulting from differences in how discrete the in-

terval boundaries of social status are relative to number."[98]

An explanation is this result is further provided by a study showing that social status and numbers comparisons have distinct and overlapping neuronal representations with the human inferior parietal cortex.[99]

8. WILL IT BE CLASS VERSUS STATUS OR LIFE CHANCES VERSUS LIFE CHOICES?

Class and status are related, but different, forms of social stratification. One can easily define class as societal groups made of individuals who accept each other as status equal. Nonetheless, class and status remain two different forms of social stratification.

Let's start with class. As defined by Weber, class refers to the category of humans who:

(1) have in common a specific causal component of their life chances in so far as

(2) this component is represented exclusively by economic interests in the possession of goods and opportunities for income, and,

(3) the component is represented under conditions of the commodity or labor market.[100]

Therefore, the class structure is formed by the social relations of economic life in general and the relation in labor markets and production units in particular. Where the sphere of social interaction is economic, the category that locates individuals within the distribution of power is class. So, class structure is a structure of inequality.

Status on the other hand refers to groups that are held together by notion of proper lifestyles and the social esteem and honor accorded to them by others. It is therefore a structure of relations of perceived, and in some degree, accepted social superiority, equality, and inferiority among individuals irrespective of economic structure. Therefore, where the sphere of social interaction is communal, the category that locates individuals within the distribution of power is status group. So, when people speak of **"class distinctions"**, **"class barriers"**, or **"class consciousness"**, they are referring to distinction of status and to status exclusiveness and sensitivity.

Occupation can be seen as one of the most salient positional characteristics to which status attaches in modern societies. A study examining the status order in contemporary British society shows a relationship between the hierarchy of occupations and status.[101] In general, the authors found that occupations requiring working with symbols and perhaps people, and especially professional occupations, confer highest status, while those that require working directly with material things confer the lowest status. At a more detailed level, they found that managers employed in a more blue-collar milieu in industry or trade tend to rank lower than managers, or indeed to rank lower than even routine administrative employees, who work in an entirely white-collar milieu. They further found occupations that require working with both people and things-such as many occupations in the now expanding service sector-typically have intermediate status rankings.[102]

It appears from the above discussion that class is a matter of dealing with **life chances**, while status is a matter of dealing with **life choices**. Social class is expected to have important consequences for individuals' life chances; while status would most likely be related to cultural consumption and to individuals' life choices. For a good differentiation between class and status, note the following observation:

> "Whereas status groups and socials orders bound together by a common lifestyle and habitus are typically integrated, communal groups (that is *gemeinschaft* relationships), economic class refers to the large aggregates of individuals defined and determined by their relationship to the means of production."[103]

9. IS INFORMAL STATUS PREFERRED TO FORMAL STATUS?

The general interest in status is commonly about **formal status**, referring to a formal position or rank in an organizational hierarchy.[104] The general belief is that formal status matters. The reality is that formal structures have became less prominent, in favor of emerging status hierarchies or informal status processes, in addition and including the status organizing processes of ad hoc groups[105], and the complexities of organizations as distinctive social systems.[106]

Informal status is the end result of evaluations made of the worth, prestige, honor, or respect of actors.[107] The informal value or status of an individual is determined by the group's expectations of the individual's contribution to the group's goals.[108] It is different from power as status often brings power, while power does not always bring status. In fact, one may imagine power equal with status in small task-focused groups while in organizations it is a function of not only informal status but also such factors as formal position, membership in powerful organizational units, or position in social network. One can also imagine a potential connection of an individual's status of an individual with his/her position in a social network. Further, there may be situations where individuals who have high informal status are lacking power in social networks, and where individuals well placed in a social network fail to have a high informal status.

What, then, is the role of informal status in social groups? The essential role of the person with a high informal status is to promote a group's success. A failure to do so results in a low informal status ranking. The high informal status individual is given visible awards including more control over interaction pattern and resources, more opportunities, and more social and material support.[109] He or she does not, however, have the responsibilities given to those holding high formal status, who still seem to be making a strong contribution to the group: "...high political status create an undifferentiated total impression of 'greatness'".[110] This may explain why high formal status is generally viewed by individuals as preferable to high informal status even though, in fact, it is the tenure, and skills of the informal status group which facilitates the completion of important tasks. The end result is that people will seek the high informal status group for information or advice, to pass along ideas, or simply to seek their companionship.[111]

Individuals will seek formal status for entitlements and privileges. But, the respect, prominence and influence is generally given to those holding informal status and able to get things done. It seems that in groups or organizations, it may be preferable for self actualization to have informal rather than formal status when those holding informal status are the competent group. It is a fact of life that organizations are full with people holding titles that imply a formal status and responsibilities while in fact the job is being done by competent people, not holding titles, but who are key to task completion. With times, and recognition from peers, such people are recognized for their performance and acquire the respect, prominence and influence that comes with informal status. Eventually, individuals holding informal status need to be officially recognized with a formal status and title to maintain a productive atmosphere in the group or organizations. The transfer from informal to formal status is imperative and needs to be eventually recognized by the group organization. So, not only is informal status preferable to formal status, but it is also imperative to eventually formally recognize the people holding the informal status and convert their status to formal.

10. DO YOU NEED TO HAVE THE RIGHT PERSONALITY TO BE GOOD FOR "STATUS"?

The "Big Five" personality traits are five factors or dimensions of personality developed through lexical analysis to include **openness, conscientiousness, extraversion, agreeableness, and neuroticism (OCEAN).** Openness is also referred to as intellect. They constitute a purely descriptive model of personality.[112] They are as follows:

1. Openness, which is equivalent to an individual's mental and experiential life with an appreciation of art, emotion, adventure, unusual ideas, curiosity, and a variety of experience. One may expect openness and intellect to be conducive to an exploitation of educational routes to hierarchy and status.

2. Conscientiousness is equivalent to a socially-prescribed impulse control that predisposes to show self-discipline, act dutifully, and aim for achievement. One may expect conscientiousness to be conducive to upward mobility, achievement, and hard work leading to higher status.

3. Extraversion is equivalent to an approach to the social and material world with energy, positive emotions, urgency, and positive emotionality. One may expect extraversion to be a value characteristic that will lead to higher status.

4. Agreeableness is equivalent to the tendency to be compassionate and cooperative rather than suspicious and antagonistic to others. The

potential link of agreeableness to status calls for three hypotheses. The first states that agreeableness is positively linked to status as **"nice guys finish first"**. The hypothesis states that there is a negative link as **"nice guys finish last"**. The hypothesis is a combination of the two previous hypotheses, leading to a quadratic relation in the shape of an inverted U- function. Too much or too little is not good for status, while a moderate level is best for status attainment.

5. Neuroticism is equivalent to negative emotionality, including vulnerability to stress, anxiety, depression, and negative self-conscious emotions, such as guilt, shame, and embarrassment. One may easily suggest that neuroticism will be detrimental to status attainment.

Do these personality traits predict status? Two theoretical perspectives on the origin of face-to-face status offer different rationales for the question.

The first perspective suggests that the origin of status is in the individual, with status resulting from the individual's personality characteristics.[113] Basically, personality characteristics predispose the individual to strive for status and devise an appropriate strategy to reach it. It is a case of **proactive person-environment** where the individual selects and shapes his or her own social environment.[114]

The second perspective suggests that the origin of status is in the environment, with status resulting from the group's collective judgments and decisions on who should get status.[115] The group awards the status position on the basis of positive and negative characteristics possessed by the individual being ranked. It is a case of **evocative person-environment interaction** where different status positions are assigned to different individuals.[116]

The two perspectives imply that the individual may possess certain personality traits, which added to other factors will help determine the group's status evaluation of the individual. The question becomes to determine the group's status evaluation based on the personality traits and factors that allow an individual to attain status. The findings are as follows:

1. **Status attainment**, as represented by extrinsic career success, was linked to low neuroticism, high extraversion, low agreeableness, and high conscientiousness.[117]

2. Greater status attainment in women was linked to individuality, a trait linked with striving to act in one's own interests rather than those of others.[118]

3. Peer rating of status in social groups (specifically, fraternity, sorority, and dormitories) was linked to the Big Five personality traits and physical attractiveness.[119] High extraversion substantially predicted elevated status for both sexes. High neuroticism, incompatible with male gender norms, predicted lower status in men. Physical attractiveness and emotional stability predicted higher status only in men.

4. Holding leadership positions was linked to **social potency** and achievement.[120]

5. Leadership, rather than status, was linked to the Big Five personality dimensions, namely high conscientiousness, agreeableness, and extraversion and low neuroticism.[121]

6. Leadership emergence is linked positively to extraversion, conscientiousness, and openness, and low neuroticism.[122]

7. Using multiple indices of status, the research shows the power motive **"hope for power"** to be predictive of holding executive offices; extraversion and consciousness to predict peer-ratings of social influence; extraversion, emotional stability, and dominance to be related to subjective beliefs of personal power and influence.[123]

11. IS WHAT YOU THINK OF YOUR STATUS MORE IMPORTANT THAN THE CARDS YOU WERE DEALT?

Early life status (e.g. mother's education), **ascribed status** (e.g., gender, race), **achieved status** (e.g. education, occupation), and **observed behaviors** (e.g., one's manner of speaking, style of dress) are generally used as important markers and determinants of how much objective status an individual should have. An individual's evaluation of his or her own status is the perceived social position or **subjective social status**. The MacArthur Network on SES and Health offered a measure of subjective social status designed to capture individuals' sense of their place in the social ladder while taking into account standing on multiple dimensions of socioeconomic status and social position. The MacArthur Scale of Subjective Social Status presents a "social ladder" and asks the individuals to place an "X" on the rung on which they feel they stand. There are two versions of the ladder, one related to traditional SES indicators **(SES ladder)** and the second related to one's community **(community ladder).**

The subjective social status' importance has grown as more evidence was found about its stronger relationship with health than the objective social status indicators. The evidence shows subjective social status to be a composite measure of SES that includes aspects such as occupation and income,[124] a cognitive average of standard markers of SES, and elements representing an assessment of current and future prospects.[125] A question arises regarding the reasons for the importance of the subjective social status, especially given that it is as strong, if not a stronger, predictor of health outcomes than objective social status.

An interesting research result was provided by the examination of the neural differences that might occur as a function of perceived social status.[126] Using structural neuroimaging techniques to investigate whether certain neural regions vary in size as a function of **"perceived social standing"**, a study found that self reported status correlated with gray matter in only one region of the entire brain, the perigenual anterior singular cortex (pACC).[127] It varied in size depending on perceived social standing. The same neural region had been found in another study to correlate with a serotonin-related gene.[128] This might explain earlier findings on serotonin levels and social status in mammals, where those with lower serotonergic functioning have lower social status, and where those with higher serotonergic functioning tend to have higher social status.[129]

The morale of the whole story is that what you think is your status is far more important than the cards you were dealt Your thoughts about your own social status are far more important than factors such as the socioeconomic class into which you were born.

12. IS IT ABOUT STATUS OR WEALTH?

Questions naturally arise as to whether people's intentions are to signal status, signal wealth or signal both to others in society. Research suggests the following:

1. A first line of research indicates that people care about status because it serves as a signal of non-observable abilities.[130] It can also be maintained that status enhancing goods are **"money burning"** goods that leads to a perfect revelation of the agents' abilities over the long run. Suggestions were made to the effect that individuals can a) signal their ability to employers by undertaking some seemingly irrelevant but costly activities interpreted as status consumption,[131] or social culture,[132] or b) "burn money" on fashion to signal abilities in a **"dating game"**.[133]

2. Another line of research maintains that people want to signal wealth because high relative wealth leads to preferential treatment in social contacts. For example, it is maintained that people care about relative wealth because it affects mating.[134] Being the top male in females' ranking assures the best match a male can get which justifies the concern about relative social position. In addition, high relative wealth leads to wealthier mates and higher consumption, with consumption serving now as a signal of wealth.[135] As **Madonna** said in her **"Material Girl"** song: "**The boy with the cold cash is always Mister Right because we are**

living in a material world and I am a material girl". The excessive consumption and the resulting sub-optimal saving depends in fact on the specific details and timing of the **'conspicuous consumption race'**. It was shown that if the signaling is typically done late in the life cycle, conspicuous consumption actually encourage savings.[136] The hidden rationale for the conspicuous consumption is to insure that any expenditure, aimed at raising the status of some people, is intended to impose an external cost and a downgrading of other people's status. Those people with the downgraded status can elect to **'ape"** the high status people by buying cheap knockoffs of expensive goods, keeping the status rivalry as a **zero-sum game** (as long as the cheap knockoffs have roughly undetectable quality).

3. A final and more correct line of research is to view the routine situation of individuals seeking to enter a club and benefit from the goods offered by the club which is available to people of wealth and from the status created by membership in the club. The process includes the individual joining the club offering a unique good and then benefiting not only from the good offered by the club but also by the status associated with the club membership. To go from joining the club to getting the status effect, the individual's wealth needs to be observed. As Frank wrote: "In societies in which economic interactions between people are important and pervasive...information about people with whom we might interact

has obvious value. It determines for example, the people we consider as potential mates, the employees we hire, those whose company we seek, and so on."[137] Given the less than perfect information on individual incomes, the individuals are reduced to over-spending on conspicuous goods to signal wealth and deserve status. This follows from the argument that individuals may be tempted to over-consume so as to reach a higher status than the one they would obtain in the case of perfect information. This behavior can be doomed to failure when people are able to correctly infer the signals about the true social situation.[138] The end result is **suboptimal consumption** without intrinsic utility.

We have as a result the absurd, recurring situation where people are overspending to signal wealth that justifies membership in exclusive clubs hoping to get the desired status associated with the membership. One may imagine Groucho Marx going through this scenario and joining this club after signaling wealth and finally wisely declaring: **"I refuse to join any club that would have me as a member:"** Marx definitively shows his understanding that the wealth he signaled through joining the club does not guarantee getting the desired social status.

13. DOES THE SPIRIT OF CAPITALISM LEAD TO THE "RED QUEEN" ECONOMY?

It is generally implied that the accumulation of wealth is often taken to be solely driven by one's desire to increase consumption rewards. One may question why some rich people continue to work. This has led to the hypothesis that investors accumulate wealth not only for the sake of consumption but also for the wealth-induced social status. It essentially captures **the spirit of capitalism**. As stated by Weber:

> "Man is dominated by the making of money, by acquisition as the ultimate purpose of his life. Economic acquisition is no longer subordinated to man as the means for the satisfaction of his material needs. This reversal of what we should call the natural relationship, so irrational from a naïve point of view, is evidently a leading principle of capitalism"[139]

As also stated by Keynes:

> "...society was so framed as to throw a great part of the increased income into the control of the class least likely to consume it. The new rich...preferred the power which investment gave them to the pleasures of immediate consumption...Herein lay, in fact, the main justification of the capitalist system...And so the cake increased; But to what end was not clearly contemplated.

> Saving was for old age or their children; but this was only in theory...the virtue of the cake was that it was never to be consumed, neither by you nor by your children after you."[140]

Basically, investors will acquire wealth not just for its implied consumption, but also for its induced status. As a result, it has been argued that investors will be more conservative in risk taking and more frugal in consumption depending on their relative social standing, and stock prices will be more volatile than when the spirit of capitalism is absent.[141]

A self-defeating situation arises as a result of accumulated evidence that people tend to evaluate their own consumption in the light of the consumption of others. Basically, with everyone increasing their conspicuous consumption to improve status, any gain in status is cancelled out by similar increased expenditures of others, resulting in what may be termed Lewis Caroll's **"Red Queen"** economy, in which **"it takes all the running you can do to keep in the same place."**[142] This **"Red Queen" effect** may become more significant if income in society increases. The rationale is expressed as follows:

> "the proportion of income spent on conspicuous consumption increases and equilibrium utility falls at each level of income. Partly this is because, as a society becomes richer, those whose incomes do not grow

spend more on conspicuous consumption in an attempt to keep up."[143]

The same rational applies to organizations. Organizations facing competition will strive to improve performance and accumulate beneficial learning needed to maintain a status condition. The same learning can trigger learning from rivals and as a response more learning from the first organization holding the status title. This is a self-reinforcing process, known in evolutionary theory as the "Red Queen".[144] This co-evolution among organizations involved in an ecology of competition and learning is in fact a constant fight for status.

Status, in fact, can portend undesirable future outcomes, such as nonproductive rent seeking behaviors among high-status individuals, and potential of complacency as a result of outstripping one's peers in wealth. This has led to the observation that the "chief danger of status is that of suppressing personal development, and so causing social enfeeblement, rigidity, and ultimate decay,"[145]

14. WHAT IS IT WITH MIDDLE-STATUS PEOPLE AND CONFORMITY, CRIMINALITY AND, INNOVATION?

On may look at the status hierarchy as composed of **high-, low- and middle- status** categories. The question is, How does membership in any of these status categories determine individuals' actions in such areas as **conformity, criminality**, and **innovation?**[146]

Research findings suggests that when it comes to conformity, the force of social influence on individual judgment leads to an inverted U-shaped (IUS) relationship between status and conformity. Basically, conformity is high in the middle, yet low at the top and bottom of a status hierarchy. Low status individuals are not eager to conform. They may feel tempted to deviate from accepted routines and rituals, given that they are generally excluded from strategic decisions taken and they see their deviating actions minimized or ignored. High status individuals feel free not to conform. Given their high social acceptance, they may feel emboldened to adopt unconventional behavior.[147] [148] Their outlandish behavior in some cases may be viewed as a sign of eccentricity, encouraging them not to conform and implicitly rewarding them with the attention and the curiosity of the **"riff-raff"**. Middle status individuals value their membership in a group, yet feel insecure in that membership and that leads them to signal high conformity as a way to gain acceptance and legitimacy.[149] [150] They are tainted by the stigma of middle class conservatism and the ensuing anxiety experienced by one who aspires to a social station but fears disenfranchisement.[151]

Research suggests that when it comes to innovation, the evidence favors a U-shaped curve with high status individuals more likely to adopt innovations that interlock with prevailing group norms while low-status individuals originate counter-normative innovations.[152]

Finally, with respect to criminality, the focus of research has been on whether the relationship between either class or status and criminality is linear.[153] It would be more intuitive and more worthy of research to investigate the thesis that criminality and deviance are low in the middle but high at the top and the bottom of the status hierarchy. To see this, witness the extremes of gang activities at the low end of the hierarchy and the **Ponzi** schemes a la **Bernie Madoff** at the high end of the status hierarchy.[154]

15. DOES STATUS GIVE YOU ACCESS TO RESOURCES?

Research has pointed to the relative ease with which high-status actors acquire both tangible resources such as physical, social, and financial capital, and intangible resources such as self-efficacy and expectations states. Both types of resources elevate performance and thus, achieve social status.

With regards to the tangible resources, the ease of acquisition by higher-status actors can be illustrated in various settings:

1. In the academic field, there is an additional constraint on marginal scholars caused by the limited access to physical and human capital. As stated by Merton: "By hypothesis, some unknown actors are caught up in a process of cumulative disadvantage that removes them early from the system of scientific work and scholarship."[155]

2. In the biotechnology field, young biotech firms endorsed by high-status third parties get public funding faster than those without such endorsements[156]

3. In the legal field, higher-status firms have more bargaining power.[157]

4. In labor management, it is asserted that organizational status reduces labor costs.[158]

5. In terms of entrepreneurship, higher-prestige academic scientists are now more likely to become academic entrepreneurs.[159] This may be

due to the known fact that elite scientists are significantly better poised to attract resources necessary for doing so.[160 161]

With regards to the intangible resources, the ease of acquisition is illustrated by both self-efficacy and expectations states.[162] Higher confidence of higher-status actors, a self-efficacy situation, leads to better performance, such as for example the case of enhanced performance in standardized tests.[163] Added to the confidence and performance of higher-status actors, positive feedback leads to a virtuous cycle referred to as **"efficacy-performance spiral"**.

In terms of expectations, higher status actors are expected to perform better than lower-status actors. Whether it is a form of **labeling theory**,[164] or a form of **self-fulfilling prophecies**,[165] such expectations can result in lower-status actors having little choice but to demonstrate their marginal positions by performing poorly. This was illustrated in a study that showed being distinguished as low status among a street gang's members fostered variance in members' athletic performance, to conform to their location in the gang's pecking order.[166] under this theory, neither high- not low-status actors can deviate from the expectations if they want to avoid penalties imposed by the social group.

A worker's title is like **a status symbol**. For the status symbol to be effective in giving access to resources, it must be recognized as legitimate. In an experiment, workers performing a task were given extra responsibilities in corporations with a high status job title that was either earned on the basis of superior performance, or was unearned in the sense that it was bestowed for no apparent reasons.[167] The results of the experiment showed that the earned job title provided adequate compensation while the bestowal of an unearned job title led ultimately to a sharp performance decrement and even feelings of underpayment.

16. WHAT ARE THE HYPOTHESES ON THE LINK BETWEEN SOCIAL STATUS AND CULTURAL CONSUMPTION?

A question arises whether there is a link between social status and cultural consumption in general and taste and lifestyle in particular. Various hypotheses have been proposed as follows:

1. A first hypothesis may be labeled **the status hypothesis.** It states that social status is steadily increasing in lifestyle measurements, especially relative to the average cultural level.[168 169] People may be inclined to "consume" (attend) cultural activities such as opera, theater or ballet for example as a way of "signaling" to others who they are, and how they should be treated. Material possessions or privileges play the role of **"status symbols"**[170] Similarly, discourse about cultural consumption signals a status level to the intended audience. As stated by DiMaggio: "Subjects of conversation supplant objects of displays as bases of social evaluation."[171]The status levels vary with taste categories generally recognized as **"highbrow", "middlebrow", and "lowbrow".** An examination of the association between newspaper readership and status showed a strong and systematic association between status and newspaper readership. As stated by the authors:

> "The probability of individuals reading "highbrow" broadsheets rises with status, and at an increasing rate; the probability of their

reading "lowbrow" redtop tabloids falls with status in a more or less linear fashion; and the probability of their reading "middlebrow" tabloids first increases with status and their decreases."[172]

The status hypothesis is also known as the **"homology"** argument which indicates that cultural consumption is closely linked to status, in the sense that people with high status are more likely to prefer and consume highbrow culture while those with low status are more inclined to prefer lowbrow culture.

2. A second hypothesis states that differences in cultural consumption are just the result of differences in individual differences in **information processing capacity**.[173] The people of higher status may have on average greater information processing capacity which allows them to have a better appreciation of higher cultural forms and to have "highbrow" tastes. This follows also from the fact that cultural and other forms of consumption may have become radically **"individualized"**, reflecting individuals' free choice as they construct their personal lifestyles and identities.[174] In fact, individualization arguments contend that consumption t is not necessarily linked to status given that individuals make choices from various possibilities offered by today's highly commercialized consumer societies.

3. A third hypothesis, known as the **"status anxiety hypothesis"** maintains that the upwardly mobile may be insecure about an acquired status

and will signal their status by shunning completely lowbrow culture and embracing only highbrow forms. The upwardly mobile, as well as the downwardly mobile, may conditionally retain some of their previous lowbrow culture forms, which allows them to switch allegiance and liking of cultural forms depending on the context and then people with whom they are interacting.[175] The "status-anxiety" hypothesis can go in tandem with a **"status switching" hypothesis** or a **"culture switching hypothesis"**. As Di Maggio quips: "An upper-working class father with a white collar wife must know about sports and rock music at work, discuss politics and natural foods with his wife's friends, and instill an admiration of Brahms and Picasso in his daughter or son."[176] This is also known as the **omnivore-argument thesis** in the sense that the cultural consumption comprises not only more "highbrow" culture but more **"middlebrow"** and "**lowbrow"** culture as well, while the cultural consumption of low-status individuals tends to be largely restricted to more popular cultural forms.

17. WHAT'S CAUSING ALL THIS ANGER AND AGGRESSIVE BEHAVIOR?

A general thesis that the general primate tendency toward social hierarchy, allowing competition among group members (for food, water, sleeping sites) to be performed efficiently with as little injury or risk of injury as possible, is at the root of **status behavior**.[177] Identifying the winner of an encounter between two individuals without actual fighting naturally leads to a status hierarchy. These **status hierarchies** are generally viewed as either cooperative, goal-oriented behaviors, or as conflictual behaviors. There are, of course, negative aspects of status conflict that arises with the conflictual behaviors[178]

In fact, anger seems to be linked in people's minds with high status positions. People expect high status others to feel angry and expect angry people to be high status.[179] [180] Participants in an experiment who read a vignette about two characters believed that the character described as angry was high status, and that the character described as sad and sultry was low status. Social position may be inferred from emotional expressions as individuals with angry facial expressions were believed to be occupying more powerful social positions than individuals expressing sad facial expressions.[181]

This association between anger and high status is not only descriptive but also prescriptive. In effect, a series of four experiments, in essence, provided evidence that anger leads to status conferral in both a political and a business context, with the expression of anger seemingly interpreted as indicating that the expressor can be learned from and is competent.[182] Anger led to status and control of resources, and the end result is that both men and women find it easier to like and to admire those who demonstrate greater ability or control of resources.[183]

Among humans, many male-male conflicts with escalating violence begin with disputes over "respect" where a status challenge from an approximate equal cannot be ignored. Similarly, aggression may be used to enhance status as a way to augment an individual's ability to attract a mate. This link between aggression, status and mating has been observed primarily in nonhuman animals. Recent work shows that aggressive display by men also leads to an enhanced social status, which in turn boosts their ability to attract a mate and reproduce.[184] More specifically, for men, status motives increased direct face-to-face aggression.

18. WHAT MOTIVATES WORK: MONEY, STATUS AND/OR RESPECT?

In studying the determination of status in different societies, the primary technique was to conduct surveys asking people to rank occupations according to their prestige. It is interesting to note that the ranking of occupational status is stable over time and similar in different societies. [185] Basically, occupations requiring high levels of education and guaranteeing high income were conferred high social status. A physician is conferred a higher status than a butcher. One would expect people to choose occupations not only for the monetary rewards but also for the status associated with that occupation. The individual benefit comes not only from the wage he or she receives but also from being associated with a high status occupation.

It is widely believed that a firm motivates employees to do their best by the use of "**performance-related pay**". This belief has been successfully challenged by empirical evidence showing that rewards schemes may sometimes fail to influence employee performance, and behavioral biases ought to be included for a better appreciation and understanding of executive pay.[186] One crucial behavioral bias is the deep-rooted drive for status leading to attempts to answer two deeper questions about what fundamentally drives human ambition and effort: "Is status valued as an end that provides access to resources or rather as an end in itself? How is status seeking linked to the evolutionary history of the species?"[187]

With regards to the first question of whether status is a means to an end or an end in itself, the answer differs whether a classical and purely rational approach or an emotional and biological drive approach is used.

The classical or purely rational approach sees status as a means to entitlements to physical resources, e.g. money, real estate, fashion goods, etc. The notion is not intuitive but can be supported by evidence as high status offers more opportunities to have access to resources, influential networks and career advances. One serious implication of the classical approach suggesting that it is perhaps seriously flawed is that with the removal of resources, status drive becomes irrelevant.

The emotional and biological drive approach is based on evidence that status is an end in itself in most cases, and that status behavior is generally motivated by powerful sub-conscious drives: namely emotional and biological drives. People are willing to give up money for the nice feeling that comes with status.[188]

With regard to the second question of how is status linked to the evolutionary history of our species, the answer lies in a stylized evolutionary explanation of status. For all species, competition drives the distribution of resources. Short of a lethal battle where all the competitors may face some injuries or face new competitors, a settlement for a semi-stable status hierarchy is generally preferred as a solution. It does not eliminate the general possibility that someone will eventually pose a challenge and attempt to dislodge the alpha individual. These "primitive" status biases are also visible in humans with findings that large, tall men tend to be listened to more, offered more respect, and have on average better career progress than short, small men: e.g., the taller of the two presidential candidates have won 20 out of 23 times between 1990 and 1992.[189]

Reproductive success and high level of serotonin were also found to be associated with high status.[190] [191] It seems that the status drive is hardwired into humans.

The main implication for managers is that employees will not only pursue status as a way of getting to resources but also will actively seek status as an end in itself. Therefore, they should be using this existing drive for status as a powerful motivator serving the interests of the group and the firm. One implication is that creation of non-monetary symbols of status within the firm can provide both the firm and employees with the benefits of status seeking without the high financial costs associated with monetary rewards. This is very similar to what has been labeled the **"positional treadmill"**, where status is channeled toward criteria of effort and performance.[192] The expectation is that employees may strive to work harder on productive activities in order to enjoy a high status rank.

The possibility of using non-monetary rewards to encourage productive behavior is not limited to status seeking rewards. One interesting opinion suggests that while acknowledging that workers appreciate monetary rewards, they also get utility from what they believe that others think about them and will react favorably if offered a combination of monetary rewards and respect.[193] This is in conformity with survey results showing that workers want more than just monetary compensation and that they would welcome a kind of appreciation and recognition from their employers that convey "respect". This is also in conformity with the call in popular management books for symbolic awards. The conclusion of such survey is the development of a public recognition program with three main ingredients: personal attention, public celebration, and mementos.[194] In addition to respect, workers are known to value positively the amount of attention being paid to them,[195] as well as higher levels of supervisor trust, friendship, and respect.[196]

19. WHAT'S GOING ON WITH STATUS, INVESTING, AND "KEEPING UP WITH THE JONESES"?

The rich are definitively wise about savings. The evidence is that households with higher levels of lifetime income have higher lifetime savings rates. Perhaps, the best way offered to explain this fact is that either consumers regard the accumulation of wealth as an end in itself, or unspent wealth yield a flow of services (such as power or social status) which have the same practical effect on behavior as if wealth were intrinsically desirable.[197]

With these high savings rates, one may wonder how the rich invest their money as compared to the less fortunate. The less fortunate are happy to, or are reduced to hold, rather simple portfolios of financial and real assets; often consisting of a checking/saving account plus a home and mortgage, and not much else.[198] The more fortunate or rich households tend to hold a much higher proportion of their portfolios in risky assets, with a particularly large particular concentration of net worth in their own entrepreneurial ventures.[199] One explanation is that high risk takers and households engage in high risk-high return activities, and the risk-lovers who are lucky constitute the rich.[200] Another explanation is that the capital market imperfections require entrepreneurial activities to be largely self-financed, and these same imperfections imply that entrepreneurial investment will yield high average returns.[201] This poses a dilemma as rational investors prefer an investment strategy that focuses on diversification and risk sharing while the evidence shows that rich households are holding portfolios that are poorly diversified and tend to include a larger proportion in shares in closely held businesses.[202] Basically, the investment strategy of rich households is characterized by lower diversification and higher exposure to **"idiosyncratic" risk** rather than **"aggregate risk"**. Entrepreneurs are in the same situation when they take poorly-rewarded risks despise the presence of potential alternative investments in public equity that can give them a large risk premium and the related higher level of expected rates of return on investments.

What motivates the wealthier to engage in more risk-taking behavior? The answer provided in the literature that makes sense is based on the human desire for social status and the related satisfaction brought by **"getting ahead of the Joneses"**. This idea can be traced back to Adam Smith's suggestion that at higher level of income, people value the **"social esteem"** brought on by their wealth more than the consumption of goods and services that this wealth can buy.[203] One can also use the argument made by Max Weber that love of wealth for its won sake is **the spirit of capitalism**,[204] resulting in more focus on social standing, and lower risk aversion in the portfolios of the rich. Another suggestion of the role of social class was made by Friedman and Savage when they asserted that as people move to a higher "social class" their marginal utility of wealth rises.[205] They are more willing to take great risks to separate themselves from others. What all these suggestions imply is that wealthier households care more about their social position in relation to consumption than do poor ones.

A model proposed by Roussanov suggests that the desire to "get ahead of the Joneses" is what leads to the findings that investors' aversion to idiosyncratic risk is lower than their aversion to aggregate risk.[206] The model is another confirmation of the empirical findings showing wealthier households hold a disproportionate share of risky assets, particularly private equity, and experience greater volatility in wealth and consumption growth.

This theoretical and empirical evidence that the wealthier people engage in risk taking behavior will most likely not hold in societies where the distribution of status is exogenously fixed, and thus is not necessarily closely tied to relative wealth,[207] because greater capital accumulation and the resulting high risk taking behavior is more likely to happen in a "**wealth-is-status**" context than in an "**aristocratic**" context.[208]

An interesting example of the risky behavior of wealthy investors appeared when three mutual funds created closed-end funds to take advantage of the Obama administration's toxic asset program-the same toxic assets that nearly sank U.S. banks, until taxpayers bailed them out.

Because individual investors buying these closed-end funds would run the risk of taking a beating, the belief was that only the wealthy investors will take the risk.[209]

20. DOES SOCIAL STATUS LEAD TO REPRODUCTIVE SUCCESS?

Strength and beauty, as forms of status in the animal world, are signals of reproductive success. When peacocks expend resources to grow ornate tail plumage, it is not for their own pleasure but as a way to attract peahens. Status seeking as a pervasive phenomenon and the primary force behind much of the human evolution plays the same role in human society.[210] It can definitively signal reproductive fitness and may be a magnet for attracting desirable mates.

A general accepted thesis is that humans aim for the high status that can give them a better chance at **reproductive success**. There is definitively a positive relationship between reproductive success and status or social rank in most animal populations.[211] In pre-industrial human populations, most studies show a positive relationship between male status and number of surviving offspring with male status measured as hunting ability, political status, prestige, wealth, landownership, income, power, education, social status, and rank in nobility. For a long while, having more children was more the forte of individuals of higher social standing. The most striking case is related to the finding that 0.5% of the current world population share a certain Y chromosome signature signaling the case of one male ancestor, believed to be **Genghis Khan.**

The situation has changed dramatically in modern human population as a result of the demographic transition and the availability of effective contraception.[212] The positive link between status and reproductive success has become less significant as evidence showed that high-status individuals were having fewer offspring than do low status individuals,[213] and fewer children, even if they are of higher quality, may lead to fewer genetic descendants on average.[214] With emerging lower fertility rates among elites, it appears that those with high income/wealth or high occupation/social class switched from relatively many to relatively fewer children.[215]

In addition, more evidence is emerging to indicate that male status as measured by wealth[216] and height[217] contributes to higher reproductive success. Although high-status males did not have greater achieved fertility than do low-status male, they did have greater potential for fertility as estimated by copulation frequency.[218] [219]To add to the complexity of the contemporary situation, there is evidence of between -sex differences in mate preferences, with a general female preference for equal- or higher-status males as mates, and a general male preference for younger mates.[220] The end result over time is a shrinking pool of possible mates for high-status females, expanding the pool of possible mates for high-status males, and low-status females finding more available mates than low-status males would.[221] It has been called the plight of the high-status women: well educated in their 30's, with a well- paying job and a great social life, but less likely to marry. They have been labeled as **SWANS-Strong Women Achievers, NO Spouse**. Sylvia Ann Hewlett claimed that high achieving women who were still single at age 30, had a less than 10% chance of ever marrying. She declared in her book, **Creating Life**: "Nowadays, the rule of thumb seems to be that the more successful the woman, the less likely she will find a husband or bear a child."[222] That view is shared by Maureen Dowd in her book: **Are Men Necessary**, where the award-chiever journalist writes: "I was always so proud of achieving more-succeeding in a high-powered career that would have been closed to my great-aunts. How odd, then, to find out that being a maid would have enhanced my chances with men."[223]

Social scientists at the University of Aberdeen, Bristol and Glasgow in Britain tested the IQ of 900 boys at age 11 and then checked on the rates of marriage 40 years later. In the study published in Journal of Personality and Individual Differences, they found that higher IQ increases the chances a man will marry but a high IQ causes an even greater decrease in the chances a woman will marry. Similarly, Stephanie Bown and Brian Lewis in a study published in 2004 in Evolution and Human Behavior found that males, not females, were mostly attracted to subordinate partners for high-investment activities such as marriage and dating. The interesting explanation given by the authors is that given that female infidelity is a severe reproductive threat to males only when investment is high, a preference for subordinate partners may provide adaptive benefits to males in the context of only long-term, investing relationships: not one-night stands.[224] They admit, however, that high-status females can bring more money to the marriage and have in general, contrary to popular stereotypes, an edge in looks. It seems that intelligence and body symmetry are correlated.[225]

To provide more evidence on the subject, Rosemary L. Hopcroft reexamined the relationship between status and reproductive success in the contemporary United States. She provided the following results:

1. High-income men report greater frequency of sex than all others do.

2. High-income men have more biological children than do low-income men and high-income women.

3. More educated men have more biological children than do more educated women.

4. Intelligence decreases the number of offspring and frequency of sex for men and women, a suggestion of the ability of intelligence to work against any evolved psychological predisposition toward reproductive behavior we may have,[226] and adds to the puzzle of the evolution of intelligence.

21. DOES SOCIAL STATUS MAKE YOU AN INFLUENTIAL JUROR?

Tocqueville asserted jury room interactions are "bound to have a great influence on national character."[227] As a small group, the jury allows for the collective development and recognition of symbols, communities, and identities.[228]

A basic tenet of the judicial system is that unanimous verdicts require that all jurors must concur and the disagreement by one juror can overturn all the others. One or more influential jurors can of course lead all the others to a consensus on a unanimous verdict. Back in the 1950's and prior to the **Jury Selection and Service Act of 1968** and subsequent rulings that increased diversity in jury pool, the research indicated that upper-class men do most of the talking in mock jury deliberation.[229] In addition, recognizable, external status characteristics, such as gender and social class, can restructure otherwise undifferentiated small groups.[230] In particular, on average three jurors account for more than half of the total speaking time in a deliberation and men not only speak in deliberation,[231] and men, not only speak in deliberation more than women, regardless of occupation and race,[232] but also initiate about 40% more comments than females.[233]

Now that jurors are more diverse, are they able to achieve an inclusive and egalitarian interaction, or are they still dominated by historically privileged status groups? There is ample evidence that status distinctions are still influencing participation in the jury room despite ideals of unanimity and diversity:

1. There is still a perpetuation of the situation of males speaking in deliberations more frequently than women.[234] This situation conforms to the social psychological research indicating that gender differences in mixed-sex groups shape performance expectations.[235]

2. Income levels combined with education attainment and occupation has an effect on participation in deliberation where individuals with higher occupation statuses and higher levels of education participating more than their lower status counterparts, and proprietors and clerical workers speaking more frequently than skilled and unskilled workers. One may argue that skills such as public speaking, group leadership, and logical reasoning give an upper hand to upper-class jurors in the delivery of their comments.[236]

3. More recent evidence indicates that upper-class jurors alone-not men, not whites-are regarded as most influential in jury deliberations, due to generalized expectations of their competence or their possession of skill sets that enhance jury room performance.[237] The authors make the following recommendation on the need to identify the source of the upper-class jurors' performance:

> "This will require distinguishing between the potential effects of status generalization and actual skills that are concentrated in

the upper class. What ever the source, we also need to consider more fully the legal and social implications of upper-class individuals' disproportionate influence within the jury room. Does it have an effect on patterns of verdicts for defendants of various backgrounds? How would verdict differ if influence were equally distributed by class? A perceived lack of influence by members of the lower and middle classes might result in their dissatisfaction with and distrust of the justice system."[238]

4. When mock jurors were exposed to identical cases, with only status of the defendants experimentally manipulated where jurors were led to believe that the defendants were high, average, or low status, they gave low status defendants much harsher decisions than medium and high status ones.[239] When the experiment was replicated with a manipulation of the defendant's overall characteristics, the results showed that the defendants who have been attributed with positive characteristics were treated with extremely significant leniency as compared to those with negative characteristics.[240] Another replication indicated identical results with likeable and not likeable defendants.[241]

22. WHAT ARE THE LINKS BETWEEN SOCIAL STATUS, CONSUMPTION AND MATING?

That people care about social status results in economic consequences. The concern for social status was viewed as inducing people to engage in conspicuous consumption in order to signal wealth.[242] An extreme form of such behavior is known as the **'Veblen effect'**, which happens when individuals are willing to pay higher prices for functionally equivalent goods. A distinction is made between:

(a) **'invidious comparison'**-whenever people from a higher class consume conspicuously from a lower class, and,

(b) **'pecuniary emulation'**- whenever individuals from a lower class consume conspicuously to imitate members of the upper class.

Pecuniary emulation is suggested as the primary reason that causes people to imitate the consumption standard of those above them in the income hierarchy.[243]

There are interesting implications of status through consumption:

1. There are two ways of modeling status. A first approach specifies that status arises from an individual's comparison- in terms of his instantaneous preferences- of his own consumption to some economy-wide measure of aggregate or average consumption. A second approach specifies that status arises from an agent's stock of

relative wealth, which can consist of durable physical capital, financial assets, or both. A model based on both approaches, in the sense that social status is generated by relative consumption and also depends on the stock of durable consumption.[244] At least one study appropriately indicates that an increase in the degree of status preference raises the long-run levels of durable consumption, its corresponding stock, employment, and the physical capital stock.[245]

2. The pecuniary emulation version of conspicuous consumption is equivalent to the psychological phenomenon that "what one person consumes, the other feels forced to consume as well." The question is, What happens with this desire to "keep up with the Joneses"? The suggested answer is that it can lead to a situation in which consumers continually increase their levels of consumption in an effort to out-consume their neighbors.[246] [247] With continuous increase in spending by people to defend their relative position in social standing, this aggressive search for status via conspicuous goods becomes a zero-sum game and a "positional treadmill." Finally, when consumer motivations, other than social recognition, are taken into account, the consumption act changes from a means of signaling the consumer's status to a means of achieving norm compliance.[248]

3. If conspicuous consumption of two partly-visible goods serve as a signal of dual unobserved individual attributes (wealth and wisdom), then a distinction can be made between (a) **"elite"** (smart

agents who buy the conspicuous-consumption good) and **"nouveau riches"** (rich agents who buy the conspicuous-consumption good). Given that each select group uses a signal to distinguish itself from the others, thereby allowing a social upper-class to come to light, it was shown that low income inequality and high relative importance of intellectualism are associated with an elite equilibrium while high income inequality and relative importance of materialism lead to a nouveau riche equilibrium.[249] It is basically the introduction of a cultural-conspicuous consumption product promoting the existence of an elite equilibrium that a classic conspicuous-consumption product cannot support.

4. The wealth signaling is desired as high relative wealth leads to preferential treatment in social contracts.[250] With high relative wealth, people can have a chance at wealthier mates, which is followed by even higher consumption. The end result is that wealth is not observable and conspicuous consumption leads to consumption to serve as a signal of wealth.[251] The situation for men and women at the end of the race is as follows:

> "So men compete to acquire resources and success in that competition greatly influences rank in the male status hierarchy. Women compete for the high-status men, and the women who are successful in this competition will have a high female status. Promiscuous women will tend to lose out in this competition because men's inclusive

fitness is reduced if they expend resources on protecting other men's children, unless the men are close blood relatives. The risk is not trivial. Paternity tests reveal that even today, a significant fraction of babies have a father different from the one claimed by the baby's mother to be the father."[252]

673

3O6CWB002EJ4

673

Title	QUIET: THE POWER OF INTROVERTS I
Condition	Acceptable
Location	zone 1 Aisle K Bay 9 Shelf G Item 673
Description	This is a paper back book: This book is a different release date and may have a different cover style: Used - Acceptable: All pages and the cover are intact, but shrink wrap, dust covers, or boxed set case may be missing. Pages may include limited notes, highlighting, or minor water damage but the text is readable. Item may be missing bundled media.
Source	STORE 33
SKU	3O6CWB002EJ4
ASIN	0307352153
Code	0307352153
Employee	

23. IS SOCIAL STATUS LEADING TO WELFARE ENHANCEMENT OR INEFFICIENCIES?

Is social status welfare enhancing welfare or the cause of inefficiencies?

The first argument in the literature answering this question is that people's concern for social status may not be **welfare enhancing** and may even be the cause of **inefficiencies.** The suggestion is that people's status concern lead to an under-consumption of non-positional goods while everybody over-consumes positional goods in order to "keep up with the Jones".[253] At the same time people in general and workers in particular will signal their abilities to employees by undertaking some seemingly irrelevant but costly activities interpreted as **status consumption**,[254] or **social culture**,[255] and even **"burn money"** on fashions to signal abilities in a dating game.[256] In the same vein, it was also suggested that people's status concern leads to a **"rat race of the rich"** in the form of competition over savings.[257] There is definitively a true cost to status consumption.

The second argument derives from the alternative thesis that status consumption may be interpreted as an **ability signal.**[258] People invest in status goods because they serve as a signal of their abilities. As a result, a certain type of interaction between people, referred to as complementary interaction, can induce people to care about social status as it serves as a signal of non-observable abilities. A person's investment in status is a way of insuring an interaction with high-ability people by signaling his or her own abilities. As such, status consumption can be seen as welfare-enhancing. There is the potential for an efficiency gain in the form of more efficient matching in addition to the costs of status consumption.[259] In short, status consumption generates both a cost and an efficiency gain. Thus, it can result in either welfare-enhancing or inefficiencies depending on the context.

24. CAN SOCIAL STATUS BE LINKED TO SELF-HANDICAPPING?

If a person creates specific obstacles to success, the person is engaging in s**elf-handicapping**. What most likely happens is that the person's failure is attributed to his or her lack of special abilities.One can cite the famous case of the chess grand master Deschapelles who started doubting his abilities and started offering opponents an extra pawn and an extra move for a plausible excuse for defeat and as a guarantee for extra credit when winning the match. It is a way of ascribing poor performance to other factors than the lack of ability.[260]

This behavior is generally present when the task is **"ego involving**" and failure is anticipated. One may wonder if social status is linked to self-handicapping, and if it is ,one may intuitively predict that low status individuals are more likely to engage in self-handicapping , though this prediction is actually counter to the relevant research. The relevant research on self-handicapping with implications on social status showed that:

1. A threat to self-esteem is a good antecedent to self-handicapping. It is used as way to reduce a threat to esteem.[261]

2. Self-handicapping is more pronounced when people expect the outcome of a performance to be public.[262]

3. There is a gender effect as it appears that self-handicappers are primarily male.[263]

4. People who have been amply rewarded in life but also deeply uncertain about what they had been rewarded for would likely resort to self-handicapping as they do not perceive that their rewards have been contingent on the quality of their performance. There is a basic uncertainty about personal abilities.[264]

Based on the above arguments, it was hypothesized that because high-status individuals regularly experience non-contingent-success,[265] are amply rewarded in life while wondering what they have done to deserve it, and worrying that the rewards may end, they are more likely to engage in self-handicapping.[266] More specifically, it was predicted that European American participants will self-handicap more than will African Americans, Asian Americans, or Hispanic Americans. The study showed that men (considered high-status) self-handicapped more than women (considered lower status) and that controlling for gender, Non-European Americans self-handicapped less than did European Americans, providing tentative evidence for the proposition that status processes impact self-handicapping behavior. An interesting call for more research on the impact of gender, race and assigned status on self-handicapping has the following implications:

> "If African-American men like European-American men have been socialized to bid or status by self-handicapping, then

African-American men assigned to a high-status position would self-handicap more than would African-American men assigned to a low-status position. In contrast, African-American women placed in a high-status position would not self-handicap more than would African-American women placed in a low-status position."[267]

25. SHOULD WE TAX SOCIAL STATUS?

There are definitively consumers' preferences for **position goods;** goods that affect how others view them.[268] The consumer not only care how much of the position good he or she consumes, but also how this level of consumption compares with that of other consumers. Obviously, the consumption of position goods acts as a signal and an attempt to establish a higher level of status. This situation leads, however, not only to over-consumption of those goods that convey status, but also to inefficiency in the form of a welfare loss. One way to correct the situation is the possibility of a **Pareto-improvement tax policy**, i.e., **taxing status goods**.[269] Taxes on positional goods may be Pareto optimal since they counter over-consumption and hence reduce distortions. In addition, universal benefits in cash or in-kind reduce the inefficiency of status seeking for the poor. The policy can amount to a form of **luxury tax,** with pure profits generated by the demand for status goods.[270]

The policy can also be justified by viewing the case of relativist economy where individuals' utilities are reduced by greater consumption by others. In that case, the externalities are countered by appropriate taxes.[271] [272]

A tax on status goods may not be practical due to potential rules against discriminating taxes (i.e., the bundling of status attributes with other necessary goods) and to rapid shifts in the current set of **"in-vogue"** status goods.[273] In that case, a Pareto-improving income tax may be needed, where each individual contributes a portion of their income to the public treasury which is then divided equally among all individuals.[274] The Pareto improvement is possible because the income tax acts to counter under-supply of labor while status seeking prompts them to over-supply labor in order to obtain more funds for more expenditures on status-yielding goods.

The above discussion presents the argument that taxing status goods as much as possible and redistributing it across society can be a Pareto improvement. However, it was shown that if the signal sent by the status-enhancing good is not perfect, the Pareto improvement won't take place because taxing can harm the quality of the signal reducing the number of status good brands 'available'.[275]

26. CAN SOCIAL STATUS CONTRIBUTE TO VENTURES' SUCCESS?

Social status serves as a signal of the quality and trustworthiness of a venture firm, that allows it to reduce **"alter-centric uncertainty"**; i.e., the uncertainty that potential customers, suppliers, or partners may feel about the firm.[276] It is essential to venture firms given that the investment involves a high level of uncertainty; a **"leap of faith"**.[277] Research has identified various situations on the centrality of status in the venture field:

1. Endorsement by a high social status venture capitalist enhances a venture's chance of success by providing a signal of the venture's underlying quality to potential partners and investors.[278] [279] This is very much related to the notion that affiliations are a determinant of an actor's status, which serves as a signal of the actor's quality.[280] The determinant of an actor's status is the status of the actor's affiliations. At least one study provides support to the idea by showing that the number of urban elites who support a nonprofit organization or use its services is a positive predictor of that organization's future status.[281]
2. High social status venture capital firms typically attract high social status firms to investment syndicates.[282]
3. High status investors help ventures perform better subsequent to financing.[283]

4. Entrepreneurs often accept a discount in order to bring a high social status capital firm to the board, in the sense that they are willing to pay a price to be associated with higher-social status actors.[284]

5. The benefits arising from the social status of a firm in its home country are transferable as they aid the firm in entering new foreign markets.[285] They are transferable because they are part of the network advantages in social capital, best defined as "the sum of resources, actual or virtual, that accrue to an individual or group by virtue of possessing a durable network of more or less institutionalized relationships of mutual acquaintance and recognition."[286]

6. **Status volatility**- a form of **status inconsistency**- predictably affects negatively the rate of future growth of firms and shows the vulnerability of status as a source of competitive advantage in economic markets, by diminishing the positive main effect of status on organizational growth.[287]

27. IS IT POSSIBLE THAT TALL AND INTELLIGENT PEOPLE GET BEAUTIFUL MATES AND STATUS?

Research findings seem to provide an affirmative answer to the question posed in this chapter tilte:

1. It is generally maintained that high status people are taller and on average earn more than other people. General explanations focused on such factors as self esteem, social dominance, and even discrimination. Three findings offer more specific explanations. First, there is the **perception factor**. People seem to perceive high-status people to be taller than lower-status people.[288 289] Second, more than a perception, there is definitively a significant positive correlation between height or body size and status dominance.[290] Not only the tall chief is known as the **"Big Man"** in tribal villages, but also more than half of the CEOs of the Fortune 500 companies were found at one point in time to be six feet or taller,[291] and since 1776, the taller candidate has had a better chance of winning the presidential election in the U.S.[292] Finally, data from both the U.S and the U.,K showed that the height premium in earnings can be explained by childhood scores on cognitive tests and that taller adults select into occupations that have higher cognitive skill requirements and lower physical skill demands.[293]

2. It is generally maintained that intelligent men are more likely to occupy higher status positions than less intelligent men, where intelligence is what psychometricians call **general intelligence** or **the g factor**.[294] Men who occupy higher status positions are found to be more intelligent,[295] and there was a monotonic relationship between occupational prestige and mean IQ.[296] [297] More interestingly, the sons whose IQs were higher than their fathers' tended to be upwardly mobile, while those whose IQs were lower than their fathers' tended to be downwardly mobile.[298] [299]

3. It is generally maintained that higher-status men are more likely to mate with more beautiful women than lower status men. There is, in fact, ample evidence about the **assortative mating** between high-status men and physically attractive women. Examples follow:

a. In most cultures, men prefer physically attractive women as their mates while women prefer wealthy men of high status as their mates.[300]

b. Experiments show men preferring to mate with physically attractive women and women preferring to mate with socially dominant men.[301] [302] [303]

c. Where the caste system calls for a strict rule of **endogamy, hypergamy** where women from lower castes marry men from higher castes, the women are always physically attractive.[304]

d. Women's physical attractiveness has a strong effect on the husband's occupational status,[305] while the effect being the strongest among women from working-class families.[306]

e. Upward mobile women are more physically attractive to others[307] and, relative to average-looking women, below-average women are married to men with significantly less education.[308]

28. DOES RACE SHAPE SOCIAL STATUS OR DOES SOCIAL STATUS SHAPE RACE?

The general assumption is that race shapes social status. Those who are lucky to belong to the valued populations are more likely to have better access to rewards of society than those who belong to less valued populations.[309] A visible result of this racial inequality is the relatively large gaps in social, physical, mental, and material well-being between both groups.[310] Another visible result is the perception of race as a fixed characteristic. This last result is based on the biological thesis that views races as having different "bloods", "humans", or other bodily fluids.[311] To escape the consequences of racial changes such as **"passing", "whitening", and "mobility and stability".** Passing refers to the situation when individuals try to change racial membership by adopting a presentation of self to conform to identity features of a higher social status group. A New York Times book critic tried to "pass" as white while in fact he came from a Louisiana Creole family.[312] Whitening is when an individual who has reached a higher status is classified in a higher racial status by others as a courtesy. For example, interviewers are found to more likely "whiten" dark-skinned individuals of higher socioeconomic status than the individuals are to whiten themselves. Mobility and stability refer to the recursive situation where white people appear to be more successful in part because successful people become white and black people appear to be more criminal, unemployable in part because criminal and unemployed become black.

Person perception and stereotypical associations are a result of racial identification processes. The perception research shows that people classify faces by race, even before considering age, gender, or emotion, followed by activities in parts of the brain (the amygdale) known to control for threat or a threat response. The research even suggests that face shape, skin tone, and hair markers are used to make racial categorization decisions.[313]

The stereotypical association research suggests an association of whites with generally positive traits and black with negative traits,[314] **skin tone** with variations in positive and negative evaluation,[315] and differences in **amygdale activity**,[316] and some **"subtyping"** where lower-class blacks are described as black while middle-class blacks are described as middle-class.[317]

All the above discussion is based on the premises that race shape status and that race is a fixed part of identity, a trait that is set at the moment of conception and stays unchanged for life. These premises were successfully challenged with a view of social status shaping racial identity and race as much a flexible indicator of our social standing as it is a reflection of our biology.[318] The study relied on data from the National Longitudinal Survey of Youth, by interviewing a group of about 12,000

Americans from 1979 to 2002, classifying them as "White", "Black", or "Other", and allowing them to identify themselves by describing their "origin or descent". The data includes a racial classification by interviewers and racial identification by the subjects. The results show the following:

a) People who were classified as white in a given year were less likely to be seen in the same way if their social status changed through a job loss, incarceration, or a dip in their income below the poverty line,

b) People who were classified as black in a given year were more likely to be viewed the same way if they were imprisoned, unemployed or poor, and,

c) The subjects themselves were more likely to switch their racial identity depending on their status, and to the same degree as the interviewers did.

The results suggest that race perceptions change over time and in response to changes in social position, and this pattern holds for both self-identification and classification by others. They contradict the thesis that races and racial differences are the result of biological differences. The results also suggest race not as a fixed entity purely determined by birth, but a flexible one, settled by a tug-of-war between different possible classifications. The authors provide the following suggestion:

> "This suggests that we think of social status not only as drawing racial boundaries

between people, but also within people. The framework suggests social status not only defines racial boundaries that put people in different groups, but also social factors are also defining boundaries with a particular individual as their circumstances change over time."[319]

29. CAN INGRATIATION LEAD TO A FORMAL STATUS IN CORPORATIONS?

Formal status in a corporation is governed by the institutional structure in the form of job levels, ranks, or titles. It can be reached the usual way by excelling in the job. It can also be reached by sticking with the company for a long time,[320] using political connections,[321] or just going to another corporation.[322] It can also be obtained through **ingratiation,** that can be defined as a pattern of interpersonal influence behavior that serves to "enhance one's interpersonal attractiveness" or "gain favor" with another person.[323] Ingratiation behavior includes opinion conformity, or verbal statements that validate an opinion held by another person, other-enhancement or flattery, and favor rendering.[324] It is an act of submission or deference to another person.Findings of a study investigating interpersonal influence behavior as a substitute for elite credentials and majority status in obtaining board appointments found that top managers that engage in ingratiatory behavior toward their CEO, with ingratiation comprising flattery, opinion conformity, and favor-rendering, will be more likely to receive board appointments at other firms where the CEO is indirectly connected in the board interlock network.[325] The results also suggest that interpersonal influence behavior substitutes to some degree for the advantages of an elite background or demographic majority status.

It seems that one way to climb to the boardroom is for the lower status individuals to engage in a higher level of interpersonal influence behavior. As stated by the authors:

> .."interpersonal influence from ingratiation can substitute to some extent for the social capital provided by an upper class background, attendance at elite educational institutions, or membership in prestigious social clubs."[326]

The level of status between the ingratiatory and the target are important as low status people appear more inclined to self-presentation, i.e., presenting their own attributes in a manner to please the target. In fact, it may be stated that high status people will be more modest when induced to become ingratiating, while low-status individuals will be more self-enhancing but only in predictable ways.[327]

30. WHO PERCEIVES DISCRIMINATION? IS IT LOW- OR HIGH-STATUS PEOPLE?

Discrimination towards an individual or a group is the result of a behavior or attitudes based on class or a category other than individual merit that reflects explicit prejudice. It can be direct or subtle. Discrimination involves essentially the unjust treatment of those who have lower status and less power by those who hold more power and higher status in society, resulting in a curtailment or denial of rights of persons on the grounds of their social status or race or origin. The Human Rights Committee of the U.N. defines discrimination as:

> "Any distinction, exclusion, restriction, or preference which is based on any ground such as race, sex, language, religion, political, or other opinion, national or social origin, property, birth or other status, and which has a the purpose or effect of nullifying or impairing the recognition, enjoyment or exercise by all persons, on an equal footing, of all rights and freedoms.

It is essentially a recognition of power relations and status. All social categories that organize social relations (e.g. gender, occupations, and ethnicity) are also **status-valued categories.**[328] Some are considered as **high-status categories** while others are perceived as **low-status categories**. Because discrimination is about power and status, the members of the low-status categories bear the brunt of prejudice, negative stereotypes and discrimination. It begs the question of when a member of status-valued category experiences discrimination. Several theories and related findings provide some answers:

1. **The vigilance hypothesis** holds that as a result of frequent encounters with prejudice, members of low-status groups are more vigilant than members of high-status groups to signs of prejudice in their social encounters.[329] This may explain why cognitions that are repeatedly primed are more likely to be activated in ambiguous circumstances.[330] It also explains why prejudice is generally more central and accessible for members of traditionally oppressed groups than it is for other individuals.[331]

2. **The attributional ambiguity hypothesis** holds that members of chronically low-status groups are highly aware of the negative stereotypes others hold of their group and of their potential of being a target of prejudice in encounters with members of high status groups.[332] This may explain why members of low–status groups are more likely than members of high-status groups to report on surveys that they have been victims of discrimination.[333]

3. **The minimization perspective** holds that members of low-status groups minimize the extent to which they personally have been victims of discrimination relative to high-status groups, given that

attributions to discrimination are more psychologically costly for members of low-status groups than for members of high-status groups. In effect, attributions to discrimination reflect chronic, pervasive experiences rather than isolated occurrences.[334]

4. The status-legitimacy hypothesis holds that the more members of low-status groups endorse the ideology of individual mobility, the less likely they are to attribute negative outcomes from higher-status group members to discrimination. In contrast, the more members of high-status groups endorse individual mobility, the more likely they are to attribute negative outcomes from higher-status group's members to discrimination.[335] The hypothesis was supported among members of different high-status (European American men) and low-status (African Americans, Latino Americans, and women) groups. More specifically, members of a lower-status group who were rejected by a member of a higher-status group were significantly less likely to attribute rejection to discrimination the more they endorse the ideology of individual mobility. Endorsing legitimizing ideologies may lead members of low-status groups to perceive objectively unfair and unjust situations as fair, and may inhibit social change.

> This result about the impact of group status and status-legitimacy beliefs on attributions to discrimination within intergroup encounters may explain why beliefs about the legitimacy of group status differences also

shape other "**copying**" processes among members of low-status groups, including **selective valuing**,[336] **social comparisons**,[337] **group identification**,[338] and collective **action.**[339]

31. WHO IS ENDORSING LEGITIMIZING IDEOLOGIES?

The belief that the U.S. is a land of opportunity, where individuals are personally responsible for their social roles and positions and where the overall system of equality is equitable and fair, is an example of a **legitimizing ideology proper to the U.S. context**. It sustains the perception that the social system is just and fair, and justifies at the same time the hierarchical and unequal relationships among American social groups. Such groups hold power to legitimize social and personal inequality through their collective endorsement within the U.S. culture.[340] There are **collective representations.**[341] It begs the question as to who is benefiting from legitimizing ideologies. It should not be surprising to find that:

1. **Status-legitimizing ideologies** are more strongly endorsed by those occupying high positions in the social hierarchy than those who score low in the hierarchy.[342]
2. Individuals who are highly prejudiced are more in favor of status-legitimizing ideologies.[343]
3. Individuals high in social dominance orientation are strongly endorsing status-legitimizing ideologies.[344]

This does not stop those most disadvantaged in society from endorsing status-legitimizing ideologies.[345] The belief that status hierarchies are permeable is a primary determinant of the behavior of disadvantaged groups.[346] The disadvantaged people are likely to accept unjust status hierarchies and less likely to engage in collective actions if there is a perception of even a slight possibility of individual mobility based on merit.[347]

More interesting about the behavior of low-status groups are findings of a set of studies showing the tendency to devalue group failure is moderated by the relative status of one's ingroup status and the perceived legitimacy of that status.[348] Basically, when the status hierarchy is seen as legitimate, members of higher status groups devalue domains in which lower status groups excel, while members of lower status actually value domains in which higher status groups excel. It is important to note that if the status hierarchy defining the groups is delegitimized, members of low status groups do devalue domains in which higher status group excel.

32. DO YOU HAVE TO CHECK YOUR TESTOSTERONE LEVEL BEFORE TRYING FOR A BETTER COGNITIVE PERFORMANCE OR GOING FOR A HIGHER STATUS?

Why should you worry about testosterone levels when it comes to status and how do both affect cognition and attitudes? To answer these questions, let's start with the evidence on the role played by individual differences in testosterone levels when these levels have been associated with higher performance on spatial tests, and lower performance on verbal tests.[349] It can be explained by the assumption that the testosterone level influences cognition neuroanatomically, by shaping developing brain structures and/or by activating these structures after puberty.[350] An alternative explanation, known as the **Wingfield's challenge hypothesis**, led to a body of research arguing that the link between testosterone and cognitive performance is moderated by the individual's status in a given situation, given that testosterone only influences social behavior when status is threatened or challenged.[351] Basically, it was shown mainly in both human and nonhuman settings that individuals higher in testosterone level are more likely to intervene in order to achieve, maintain, and enhance status.[352] Testosterone levels predict behavior only when status is threatened. Winning status battles leads to an increase in testosterone levels and the winners will most likely start the next status battle with a higher level of testosterone. It is known as the **reciprocal model of testosterone and status**.[353]

Similarly, individuals with a high testosterone level are more likely to react to angry faces and are more likely to be successful at regaining status in contexts involving a physical challenge and where dominance must be regained through physical means.[354]

The question remains to know what the role of status and testosterone is when status must be regained through cognitive performance. Three research findings provide relevant answers to the question:

1. The first study starts with the assumption that a stereotype is a statement about status and finds the level of testosterone, as a factor associated with status-seeking and status-protection, will moderate the relationship between the stereotype threat and the performance.[355] Basically, given the positive relationship between baseline testosterone and **status sensitivity**, it will be expected that high testosterone levels in males and females would amplify existing performance expectations when gender based math-performance stereotype was primed. The results of the experiment showed that females high in testosterone performed poorly on a math test when a negative performance stereotype was primed while males high in testosterone excelled on math test when a positive performance stereotype was primed. Obviously, stereotype-based performance ef-

fects occur as a result of a fundamental desire to maintain or enhance one's social status.

2. The second study intended to show that individual differences in testosterone predict performance on spatial and verbal tests when status is in jeopardy.[356] The results showed that in a high-status position, high testosterone individuals performed well on both tests and blood pressure dropped, while in a low-status position, high testosterone individuals performed relatively poorly on both tests, and blood pressure did not change. Thus differences in the cognitive performance are primarily due to the interaction between testosterone and the social situation.

3. The third study investigated the mismatch effect that occurs when testosterone level and status level are at odds.[357] The findings show that low testosterone individuals reported greater emotional arousal, focused more on their status, and showed worse cognitive functioning in a high-status position, while high testosterone individuals show this pattern in a low-status position. Basically, it is better to check on the testosterone level before attempting a promotion to a higher status.

33. HOW TO REIN IN THE MATTHEW EFFECT

The **Matthew effect** was derived from **Saint Matthew's Gospel** (25:29): "For unto every one that hath shall be given, and he shall have abundance: but for him that hath not shall be taken away even that which he hath." In sociology, it is used to describe the phenomenon that **"the rich get richer and the poor get poorer."** Basically, more power or capital is gained by those who have power or capital and leverage well those resources. In the sociology of science, it was used to describe the sharp difference in recognition accorded high-and low-status scientists for comparable advantage, by which high-status scientists enjoy positive feedback between intangible and tangible resources, and thus ultimately end up with a much larger share of the rewards.[358]

The implication is that higher-status individuals get better rewards for the performance on a given task at a given level of quality than lower-status individuals performing the same task. It also implies that higher-status people will go on with much higher status and collect even larger advantages. One may ask whether it is really possible for any competitive system to allow status-based advantages to go on unabated, and nearly be monopolized by a single elite. In other words, what reins in the Matthew effect? Several arguments may be used to explain limits on high-status individuals' opportunities to multiply their resources without bound:

1. A model of status hierarchies suggests three primary suppositions: actors desire to associate with high-status alters; they desire to associate with alters who are likely to reciprocate their efforts to associate; and they are constrained in the volume of associations they can establish.[359] It is obvious from the arguments that there is a) a limit to the number of associations elites can establish, and b) the potential that marginal individuals will not seek out those who fail to reciprocate. Both arguments put a check on the Matthew Effect.

2. It is obvious that physical and normative constraints will put a check on the Matthew Effect, unless higher-status individuals were able to delegate their activities to others and still gain recognition for the successful outcomes.[360] Such form of delegation, being counterfactual, argues for exogenous factors inhibiting the Matthew Effect.

3. A check on the Matthew Effect is also evident in the potential case of low-status consumers expressing distaste for the **"slumming"** or **"carpet bagging"** by high-status producers because they may be regarded as either overqualified for low-status niches or not sufficiently committed to serving the niche.[361]

4. Whether the Matthew Effect either operates without bound or is circumscribed may depend on the degree to which status diffuses through social relations.[362] It has been shown analytically that the Matthew Effect is checked in **"porous"** systems

(where status diffuses) but operates freely in **"insulated"** systems (where status is contained). In a porous system, leaders with **"genuine charisma"** are able to transform others and create interestingly affective and personal social networks. In such systems, individuals' status levels are strongly influenced by the status levels of those deferring to them and eventually the top-ranked individual monopolizes all the status available. Therefore, in a porous system, elites endorsing others reduce their chances of accumulating ever-greater status advantages. This may explain a) the known paradox of leaders naming heirs apparent after extolling their virtues in public, and b) leaders populating their inner circles with lower-status individuals or individuals who cannot surpass them in status. Just think why eunuchs are chosen to guard the harems.[363]

34. WOULD YOU SIDE WITH MATTHEW OR MARK WHEN IT COMES TO SOCIAL STATUS?

Let's first recapitulate the **"Matthew Effect"** before introducing the **"Mark Effect"** and contrasting both effects.

Matthew 25:29 states: "For unto every one that hath shall be given, and he shall have abundance: but for him that hath not shall be taken away even that which he hath." The Matthew Effect originated in a reference to the fact that high-status researchers accumulate more credit than the low-status researchers for the same work, and end up with most of the resources.[364] It implies that investment should be made in high-status individuals as to widen the distribution of awards. Rewarding the high-status individuals is expected to not only motivate the best researchers but creates new avenues of research, and new paradigms that will benefit the entire system by putting it on the right scientific track. This unequal distribution of intangible rewards is expected to increase the social welfare, measured as the aggregate profitability or surplus of a social system. The main strategy is therefore to put the excess resources in the elites' hands and to witness the social welfare grow.

The "Mark Effect" is the result of **Mark 10:31** statement: "But many that are first shall be last; and the last first." It may be interpreted as a call for the granting of excess resources to the status-poor from the status-rich. The Mark Effect may be viewed as denoting **redistributive intervention.**[365] Subsidies are to flow to marginalized actors that are effectively feeling relative deprivation, and having negative reactions to the system-wide inequality. In effect, these negative feelings are known to lead to lower job satisfaction,[366] conspicuous waste, social conflict, acts of sabotage, and diminished health. At a more general level, inequality is found to be associated with higher mortality rates, diminished trust, social unrest, and lower satisfaction.

The question becomes to determine the conditions under which either the Matthew Effect or the Mark Effect are conducive to a betterment of individuals and to an increase in social welfare. Should we push excess resources to elite individuals, and thus potentially widen the distribution of rewards as advocated by the Matthew effect, or should we direct the excess resources to marginal individuals, and thus tighten the distribution of rewards through engaging in redistribution? A formal model of status-based competition that contrasts the two competing alternatives found that:

a) the Mark Effect is best for the welfare of **"closed"** tournaments, and therefore does not attract the attention and resources of an external audience, and,

b) the Matthew Effect is best for **"open"** contests that enjoy high status relative to other status contests, and therefore rivet the attention and attract the resources of an external public.[367]

But would the Mark Effect be allowed to go on? One may conceive of situations in which elite actors, insisting on the Matthew Effect, will kill the Mark Effect. One may also view possibilities where elites may allow the Mark effect to persist such as:

a) when elites will need marginal individuals to stay in the game,[368]

b) when elites allow the Mark Effect as a way of hedging and fishing for new superstars; and,

c) when elites are inclined to support redistribution as a result of egalitarian and social pressures.[369] [370]

35. DOES RELATIVE STATUS AFFECT RISKY DECISION MAKING BY MEN.

Evidence on the value of status is equivalent to evidence on the effort expended by people to attain status.Such concern with **relative status** is pervasive in virtually all societies.

If there are computational systems intended to regulate intra-sexual competition, then their design should be sexually dysmorphic. It appears that in most cultures women prefer men with higher status and access to culturally-valued resources as mates.[371] Not surprisingly, men are not that keen on the variations in the status and resources of women.[372] The expected consequence is that status gained through access to culturally-valued resources is central to the inter-sexual competition among men and women.[373]

Relative social status will then regulate human behavior and especially men's behavior. It affects men's motivations given that access to culturally important resources is a locus of intra-sexual competition and a determinant of status and a risky endeavor.[374]

What would be the behavior of men trying to recoup a monetary loss when faced with both a high risk/high gain option and a no-risk/low gain option? The results of one study show that men who thought others of equal status were viewing and evaluating their decisions were more likely to favor a high-risk/high option of recouping a monetary loss over a no risk/low option with equal expected value.[375] Thus, relevant status affects men's motivations for risk in relevant domains. As stated by the authors:

> "The results are consistent with the view that men, losing resources is a cue signaling an increased risk of being challenged by a competitor close in rank. Men imagining a scenario in which they had lost resources chose the risky option twice as often when they believed man close in rank were going to evaluate their choices, compared to conditions in which they believed their putative evaluations were distant in rank."[376]

36. IS EXPECTATION CONFIRMATION A RESULT OF SOCIAL STATUS?

Social status implies the existence of status hierarchies going from high status to low status individuals based on their position in the hierarchy. This results in the potential for expectations in behaviors depending on the position held in the hierarchy. Such expectations are in line with research evidence:

a) Evidence on emotional expectations for high-and low-status group members shows that angry and proud people are thought of as high status whereas sad, guilty, and appreciative people are considered low status,[377]

b) Evidence on competence expectations shows that individuals of high status are seen as more influential, competent, and worthy than low status individuals.[378]

More importantly, these expectations result in **expectation confirmation** resulting from how high-versus low-status individuals being evaluated on the basis of their abilities and performance relative to expectations.[379] The expectancy confirmation process is part of the link in the chain leading from social perception to social action. It includes two processes: the first, called "**a behavior confirmation effect**", which is a kind of "**self-fulfilling prophecy**", and the second, called "**cognitive confirmation effect**", where perceivers simply selectively interpret, attribute, or recall aspects of the target person's actions in ways consistent with their expectations.[380] Impression formation seems to be determined by expectations. Whatever their status levels, people believe that thriftiness, industriousness, and intelligence increase as one ascends the class ladder. As a result, it was found that clerks rate managers more favorably on selected traits such as competence than they rate fellow clerks.[381] People tend to pressure others to rate supervisors are more competent than subordinates.[382] Finally, observers who were watching a girl taking a test, rated her abilities well above grade level when they were told that she came from a high socioeconomic background[383]

37. DOES SOCIAL STATUS MOTIVATE VOLUNTARY CONTRIBUTION?

Fundraisers would love to know all the factors that motivate individuals to give and generally opt for the strategy of approaching well-known donors first, hoping that others will naturally follow. A New York Times article mentioned that important donations followed a contribution made by Brooke Astor, a known philanthropist, "When she gave one donation to the New York Library, for example, three other major gifts- from Bill Blass, Dorothy and Lewis Cullman, and Sandra and Fred Rose- all followed, with her generosity cited as the inspiration.[384] Obviously, her high-status generated more giving, suggesting people prefer to associate with those of higher social ranking than themselves. An examination of the effect of status on voluntary contribution showed that:

a) Aggregate contributions and earnings are larger when high-status donors are solicited before, rather than after, those of low–status donors, and,

b) low-status followers are likely to **mimic** contributions by high-status leaders, and this encourages high-status leaders to continue.[385] The lead contribution by high-status individuals is central to a successful fundraising campaign.

While the above results justify the **"red carpet"** treatment given to the initial high-status donors by fundraisers, another study went further by examining the role of status acquisition as a motive for giving involuntary contributions to public goods.[386] The study shows analytically that:

a) Donations are increasing in the value they assign to status; and,

b) Individuals' contributions are increasing in the value that their opponents assign to status, reflecting donors' intense competition to gain social status.

This is another confirmation of the role of status as an individual incentive affecting donors' giving behavior.[387]

38. WHAT DOES THE ECONOMIC GROWTH RATE HAVE TO DO WITH SOCIAL STATUS?

What does the economic growth rate have to do with status?

First, individuals' choice of occupation, investment and education is affected by social status, resulting in an impact on growth. For example, the 19th century decline in England was attributed to the general disdain for entrepreneurs and the high status of the idle gentlemen.[388] It is a kind of **noblesse oblige** where with wealth, power and status come responsibilities but also the privilege of "doing nothing".

Second, activities can be classified as **"non-productive" (or "rent seeking")** or productive activities. Research results suggest that social prestige and social status structure will be conducive to more growth if attached to productive activities.[389] With differences in occupational status implying occupational wage differences among workers of the same skill, it can be argued that the larger the demand for status, the larger the wage gap and the lower the aggregate output. The argument can be taken further when it is shown that a greater emphasis on status may induce the "wrong" individuals, that is, those with low ability and high wealth to acquire schooling, causing individuals with high ability and low wealth to leave the growth-enhancing industries, a phenomenon labeled as the **"crowding-out effect"**.[390] In any case, the relative nature of social rewards implies social scarcity (e.g., only one person can be number one), leading to rent seeking and to a limit on growth.[391] In addition, social status is generally used to regulate marriage patterns, resulting also in an impact on wealth accumulation and growth.[392]

Not only economic growth is affected by status but also social costs and benefits. In effect, one way of obtaining social status is for an individual to produce **positive externalities** that are appreciated by members of society because they create a social benefit.[393] It almost goes without saying that one way of losing status is to produce **negative externalities** that create a social cost.

39. DO THE VEBLEN EFFECTS LEAD TO HIGHER PRICES FOR SOCIAL STATUS?

Veblen argued that rich people tend to engage in conspicuous consumption as a way of signaling their wealth, and in the process achieving greater social status.[394] He stated that "In order to gain and hold the esteem of men, wealth must be put in evidence, for esteem is awarded only on evidence."[395] It is the evidence of overly expensive goods that fall into "accredited canons of conspicuous consumption, the effect of which is to hold the consumer up to a standard of expensiveness and wastefulness in his consumption of goods and his employment of time and effort."[396] Veblen makes the distinction between two motives for consuming conspicuous goods: **"invidious comparison"** and **"pecuniary emulation."**

Invidious comparison involves the situation where the high status individual is willing to incur costs and engage in costly conspicuous consumption that will differentiate him from the low-status individual.

Pecuniary emulation arises from the attempt by the low status individual to engage in some form of conspicuous consumption so that he will be sought off as a member of a higher status group.

Needless to say, the high status group would not mind to over-paying in order to keep the riff-raff away (invidious comparison), making sure that the costs are high enough to discourage imitation (pecuniary emulation). This is what is termed a **Veblen effect**, where high status consumers are willing to pay a higher, and even exorbitant, price for a functionally equivalent good. To satisfy the two kinds of consumers, luxury firms offer both "**budget**" brands (sold at a price equal at least to marginal cost), and "**luxury**" brands (sold at a price above marginal cost). Basically, the market is offering products of identical quality at different prices, a higher price luxury brand to be used by the high status consumer to signal wealth and status, and a lower price "budget" brand to be used by the lower status consumer to signal their emulation efforts.

Even the **ultra-luxury market** is showing signs of adapting to this new reality by entering the "pre-owned" market. A Wall Street Journal article reported that Bentley has begun offering warranties and other programs to help its dealers sell second-hand Bentleys.[397] The key is then to maintain the price high enough to qualify as a luxury brand. As stated in the Wall Street Journal, "a BMW in every driveway might thrill investors in the short run but ultimately could dissipate the prestige that lures buyers to these luxury cars."[398] The snob value of the luxury good can only be maintained by high prices. As stated in The Economist:

> "Recently a flight broke out between big perfume houses and a clutch of British retailers who, having bought such brands as Chanel No. 5 on the "grey market," were

then reselling them for 60% below the recommended price. For some companies, like Vuitton, the solution is to restrict sales outside their own boutiques. Those that use specialist distributors must monitor them closely. Cartier has one person in Paris whose sole responsibility is to keep tabs on its watches once they leave the workshop."[399]

The ultra-luxury market is not in danger of being invaded by the "budget brand" kind of customers as a recent 2009 census data shows that the wealthiest 10 percent of Americans-those making more than $138,000 each year-earned 11.4 times the roughly $12,000 made by those living near or below the poverty line in 2008. The ratio was an increase from 11.2 in 2007 and the previous high of 11.222 in 2003.

40. IS SOCIAL STATUS LINKED TO CORRUPTION?

One has just to read the daily headlines in newspapers over the world to acept the reality that corruption is ever present in both governmental and private agencies. Based on federal public corruption convictions per 100,000 residents for the 1998-2007 period and 2007 population estimates, Illinois, my adoptive state, scored a high 502 ranking 19th among the states and Washington D. C. , while Louisiana, which has an even more storied history of corruption, ranked third. A package of legislative reforms, including expanded whistleblower protection, new limits on lobbyist gifts to lawmakers and prohibitions against state officials taking state contracts was enacted in 2007 as an attempt to reduce corruption. This intent is best expressed by U. S. Attorney Jim Letten as follows:

> "The average person out there understands now that public corruption has adversely affected his or her quality of life, whether it's the crumbling streets they drive on, the dismal state of the public school system, the crime rate or the lack of jobs....The tolerance of corruption was partly a belief that it was a way of life, that it was so entrenched and endemic that it was untouchable and unreachable. Now the average citizen believes that something can be done about it."[400]

In fact, corruption exists in all societies and has a definite influence on investment, economic growth, and the political behavior of citizens. The general consequences of corruption are the thwarting of growth and investment, and the creation of a serious obstacle to consolidate democratic institutions and open market economies. Corruption may be defined as the misuse of a public or business office for private gains. It involves transfer payments from bribe players to bureaucrats or business people. In a world in which the actions of a policy maker or bureaucrat (as well as their consequences) are partly observable to citizens, the former have incentives to appropriate parts of the latter's income. This rent seeking behavior is more likely to happen in situations characterized by low money incentives and low social status rewards. Money incentives for public servants can be classified in three categories:[401]

1. **Reservation wages**, i.e., the wages that the workers or public servants can earn elsewhere.
2. **Efficiency wages**, i.e., wages high enough to deter corruption and bribery, and solve the moral hazard problem associated with costly surveillance system needed to monitor the acceptance of bribes.
3. **Capitulation wages**, i.e., wages lower than the efficiency wages, and most likely to lead to corruption and bribery.

To any component of the above wage system can be added social rewards as incentives to reduce corruption. Analytically, it can be shown that powerful social status rewards will interact with economic incentives to determine the level of corruption.[402] Research suggests that:

1. Reservation and efficiency wages may be lowered if associated with a powerful social status reward, and the interaction may lead to a reduction in corruption.

2. The use of capitulation wages call for higher payment to compensate for the negative status effect.

The authors concluded in their analytical study that not only social rewards as an incentives for civil servants in reducing corruption, but also that a decrease in corruption produces an externality that make wage schemes which avert corruption (efficiency wages) cheaper. The author also concludes that the existence of this externality reduces the optimal level of corruption in a society the greater the power of social status, the lower the level of corruption.[403]

41. SOCIAL STATUS AND WHAT'S IN A NAME?

One may wonder what's in a name. Experiments were conducted on identifying the language of a single name in isolation or in a document written in a different language.[404] The result show how easy it is to extract data such as sex, nationality, age, and even social and economic status by looking at nothing but the name. Basically, the names offer themselves accurate language identification, and accurate prediction of a person's vital information. As stated by the author:

> "For example, depending on the language at hand, separating male from female names can range from the trivial to impossible. Names can also provide indications about age (as first names come and go in fashion), social and economic status (compare 'Paddy' and 'Patrick III'), religions, and, in general, cultural background (Rene Antonius Maria Eijkelkamp and Abdelkali Chaiat are both Dutch football players, but certain educated guesses can be made about their cultural backgrounds from their names above), etc."[405]

There are many examples in contemporary USA where the name changes were intended to convey a better social status. While the scholar and wit Milton Himmelfarb once said that "American Jews earn like Episcopalians and vote like Puerto Ricans," it is more correct to maintain that after decades of prosperity many Jews have also begun to live like Episcopalians, or at least as they imagine Episcopalians live. They have also adopted **WASPy** first names, leading to such comic nomenclatural pairings as Tyler Ginsberg, Mckenzie Rosenthal, Hunter Fefferman, and Kelly Rabinowicz."[406] Hollywood celebrities are quick to jump on the bandwagon and change their ethnic for an upgrade in social status. Here are some noteworthy examples"

Celebrity NameGiven Birth Name

1. **Woody Allen 1. Allen Stewart Konisberg**
2. **John Wayne 2. Marrion Morrison**
3. **Larry King 3. Lawrence Zeiger**
4. **Madonna 4. Madonna Louise Veronica Ciccone**
5. **Greta Garbo 5. Greta Gustafson**
6. **Giorgio Arvali 6. Ahmed Riahi-Belkaoui**

Even corporations have been known to change their names in order to impact the marketing, positioning, and awareness of a product, which is equivalent to changing its perceived social status. Her are some noteworthy examples:

Original Name Present Name

1. **Brad's Drive 1. Pepsi Cola**
2. **Backrub 2. Google**
3. **Tokyo Electron Corp, 3. Sony**
4. **Confinity 4. Paypal**
5. **FreeDiskSpace. Com 5. MySpace.com**

42. SOCIAL STATUS, AND WHAT ARE YOU LOOKING ?

Why do we feel we have to look where another person looks?

It is a fact that humans are known to follow a person's gaze. It is rather impossible for humans not to look up when they see someone staring upwards at the sky.The research suggests a rigid, non-mentalistic system of **gaze following** that is driven bottom up by the physical properties of the stimulus, such as the relation of the dark iris to the white sclera, [407]and possibly also the orientation of the head.[408] This behavior has also been observed for special species of non-human primates. In particular, primates such as chimpanzees and macaques spontaneously follow the eye gaze of con-specifics, and direction of the gaze conveys social dominance.[409] For both humans and non-humans, the gaze following is suggestive of an obligatory social reflex: a kind of reflexive attention mechanism. They were always hints in the research environment that gaze following did not have all the features of a purely reflexive action. The limits led to the exploration whether social stimuli might also play a role in such decisions. Researchers at Duke University medical center showed that low-status rhesus macaques reflexively follow the gaze of all familiar rhesus macaques, but high-status macaques selectively follow the gaze of only of other high-status monkeys.[410] It shows that gaze-following in monkeys involves reflexive and voluntary components, and that the strength of these mechanisms varies according to social status.

Basically, the social status of an individual influences the individual's deployment of social attention. One may even states that high-status monkeys ignore the interests of the riff-raff. Applied to humans, one may suggest that biological correlates of high social status, such as elevated levels of the male sex hormone testosterone, may suppress **"social vigilance"** which is high in low-status males (or females) that readily follow the gaze of others.

When individuals of high status decide to follow the gaze of low-status individuals, and to "ape" their behavior, the phenomenon has been labeled in French as **"the nostalgie de la boue"** or **"nostalgia for the mud"**; a desire for or attraction to crudity, vulgarity, depravity, etc. **("Put a duck on a lake in the middle of swans, and you'll see that he will miss his pond and end up going back there"**, said the Marquis when the former courtesan he married tries to pass herself as a lady, but cannot escape her cravings for bad tastes."Nostalgie de la boue" was the answer given by Montrichard).[411] It refers to ascribing higher spiritual values to low status individuals-a romanticism of the faraway primitive which is also the equivalent of lower status close to home. As **Freud** noted in **Civilization and its Discontents**, the civilized or high status individuals have always longed to be uncivilized and attributed greater virtues to them.

43. IS SOCIAL STATUS GENERATING BAD MANNERS?

One may ask what would be the reaction of low-status people when they witness some transgressions by high-status people. Various studies provide some answers to several awkward situations:

1.One study found that pedestrians were more likely not to obey the signals at a crosswalk when following the example of obviously high-status (e.g., wearing a suit, a tie, a hat) than following that of an offender of obviously lower status (e.g. wearing dirty, heavy cotton trousers, and a faded tee shirt).[412] These results were confirmed by another study that showed also that people tend to exhibit follow-the-leader attitudes in front of a low-status model compared to a neutral-status one.[413]

2. In a field study, either a male or female experimenter, saying "Excuse me" or not, dressed in high- or low-status clothing, cut in line in front of subjects already stepping in queues of at least 12 persons at various stores, banks, and restaurants.[414] The results showed that high-status people, compared to low-status ones, elicited less aggressive behaviors and nonverbal reactions.

3. A research study sought to determine the conditions under which an offender's status is either a harmful liability or a protective shield. One position states that these status effects are

moderated by crime magnitude, with status acting as a liability for major crimes, and a shield for minor crimes. Another position states that the status effects are moderated by the professional relatedness of a crime, with status functioning as a liability for crimes related to the offender's profession, and as a shield for crimes unrelated to the offender's profession. The results of one study showed that high status offenders were judged more harshly than low status offenders when the crime was professionally related, but low-status offenders were judged more harshly than high-status offenders when the crime was not professionally related.[415] This shows that status liability and shield effects are moderated by professional relatedness rather than by the crime magnitude.[416]

4. One study attempted to investigate any relationship between status and people's tolerance to transgressions committed by individuals with high status.[417] The study involved a subject telling an employee that he did not have enough money to buy a croissant. The subject was either impolite or polite. The results showed that the impolite request compared to the polite one did not lead to a decrease in compliance in high status conditions whereas a decrease in compliance was observed in moderate-or in low-status conditions. The authors offer the following appropriate explanation:

> "perhaps in our experiment, the polite behavior of the low status confederate had inhibited aggressive behavior of the subject

toward such group member. When the low status confederate was impolite, then a hostile reaction towards him became appropriate. When the high-status confederate was impolite, such hostile behavior consisting in refusing to help was not produced because of the traditional effect of symbolic authority of the high status people."[418]

5. An inability to formalize thinking and adequately participate in a policy debate may lead people to react with impoliteness and resort to yelling and insults. During **President Obama**'s speech in September 2009 to a joint session of Congress regarding health reform, Republican Congressman Joe Wilson (R_S.C.) yelled out **"you lie"** when the President said his health care bill would not mandate coverage for illegal immigrants. It was a clear case of a lower status person resorting to bad manners and gum-flapping as the only way to react to a much higher status person. This was unexpected as Joe Wilson is a Southerner and manners are important to Southerners, no matters what status in life one holds. **The moral character of an individual is the best marker of his or her status.**

44. WHAT DO BEDDING AND SHRUBBERY HAVE TO DO WITH SOCIAL STATUS?

A territory refers to a specific area or place in which the satisfaction of important needs or drives occurs.[419] Three types of territories may exist:

1. **Primary territories** are viewed by occupants as relatively permanent and need to be extensively personalized.
2. **Secondary territories** are those rented and may be personalized for legitimate periods of occupancy by the occupants.
3. **Public territories** are seldom personalized and sometimes only in temporary way.

The personalization of primary territories takes place by the use of demarcation, such as fences and hedges to enhance privacy, the landscaping of the yards, and installing personalization markers, such as signs and ceramics to indicate ownership.[420] The question is whether or not this territorial marking by homeowners is a function of status. One study hypothesized that as the socioeconomic status of homeowners increased, as determined by the average cost of homes, the amount of **personalization and demarcation** on and around the home also increased.[421] The results indicated that as status increased, the amount of bedding and shrubbery also increased significantly.

While these results confirm the relationships between status and territorial marking, they also confirm the following findings:

1. To occupy and defend a territory requires recognition by border markings, that are visible to other people, with for example demarcation by fences and hedges, and personalization by bedding, shrubs, and yard decorations.

2. When people's property is well-marked versus looking apparently abandoned, vandalism is less likely to occur.

3. Demarcation and personalization signals nonverbal warning to intruders, and reduce intrusion.

In short, demarcation and personalization not only act as a status signal, but also as a defensive mechanism against vandalism and intrusion. One can't help but think of an analogy with dogs using urine marking to claim territory, advertise mating ability and to support the social order. Humans, like dogs, like hierarchy and engage in marking behavior to assert status.

45. WHAT DO GENDER DIFFERENCES IN AGGRESSION HAVE TO DO WITH SOCIAL STATUS?

Social role theory assigns different social roles to men and woman[422] Women are given a role of communality while men are given a role of agency. In **Leviticus**, God told Moses that a man is worth 50 sheikels and a woman worth 30. Gender-a social construct specifying the socially and culturally prescribed roles that men and women are to follow-is dominated by the male gender. Women are also constantly reminded of their lower status and end up internalizing the inferiority status. The lower status of women is prevalent in the whole world as manifest in women being paid considerably less than men in all occupations, in their being largely confined to and concentrated in the least paying jobs in every sector, in their limited upward mobility, and in their greater family responsibilities due to divorce, abandonment, single motherhood, etc.[423]

In social psychological research on aggression, as conducted within the framework of social theory, gender differences indicated that women are less likely to engage in aggressive behavior than men, with the difference greater for physical than for psychological aggression, and more aggression is directed at men than women.[424] Women generally have lower status than men.[425] These gender differences in aggression documented in social psychological research can be accounted for by women's lower status relative to men. This was the subject of one study that confirmed that low- relative to high-status individuals were generally perceived in a manner analogous to how women relative to men are portrayed relative to men in the social psychological research.[426] As stated by the authors:

> "Relatively speaking, women are construed as low-status individuals, and men as high-status individuals. This parallel was apparent in judgments of a) anxiety, guilt, and felt harm; b) degree of aggression under mild and strong interference (provocation); c) amount of direct physical aggression; d) chosen aggression; e) felt provocation; f) general receipt of aggression, and g) general engagement in aggression."[427]

46. DOES SOCIAL STATUS DEFINE GENDER?

As stated above, **communality and agency** are core features of gender stereotypes, with communality for women referring to an emotional, interpersonal orientation and agency for men referring to an assertive, instrumental orientation. But, these gender stereotypes in terms of communality and agency fail to consider situational constraints on behavior. This applies to other stereotypes based on ethnicity or income. In the case of ethnicity, there is evidence that people perceive speakers with low-status accents as more communal, and speakers with high-status accents as more agentic.[428] In the case of income, the evidence shows that people of average means may be perceived as more communal and less agentic than their rich counterparts.[429] With regards to the impact of status on perception of communality and agency, the evidence shows that low-status individuals relative to high-status individuals were construed as more communal and less agentic. Thus, status can account for attribution of communality and agency, independent of gender.[430] [431]

The question remains to determine whether status differences between women and men can account for features of gender stereotypes other than communality and agency. Are the gender's stereotypes due to women's lower status relative to men? A study presented evidence that supports the view that women are stereotyped as more communal, higher in unmitigated communion, less agentic, and lower in unmitigated agency because of their lower status relative to men.[432] One interpretation is that status defines gender in that low status is but a component of the female stereotype, and high status is a component of the male stereotype. Another interpretation is that gender defines status in that people's perceptions of low-status individuals are largely a reflection of their concept of women or femininity. The first interpretation is in line with:

A. the view in expectation states theory of gender as a **diffuse social cue**.[433]

B. the findings that when discussing a neutral topic, traditional status roles prevailed and men displayed greater visual dominance.[434]

C. the findings that in the absence of specific status information, men are judged as more competent than women.[435]

The understanding of general gender stereotypes as reflecting status differential between men and women leads eventually to the perpetuation of women's lower status, and has been described as a **self-fulfilling prophecy**.[436] This view is explained as follows:

> "According to this view, because women are stereotyped as interpersonally sensitive and devoted to others, they are assigned (and choose) roles that require characteristics and behaviors consistent with the stereotypes. Similarly, because men are stereotyped as more assertive, instrumental,

and devoted to self, they are assigned (and choose) roles that require such characteristics and behaviors. Due to correspondence bias, when women and men display their stereotypical characteristics, and behaviors, the qualities are seen as internal dispositions of the individual, thereby confirming the stereotype. Thus, stereotypes reflect as well as perpetuate the status differential between women and men."[437]

47. WHAT DOES SOCIAL STATUS HAVE TO DO WITH WOMEN ENGAGING IN MORE MALADAPTIVE WORRY THAN MEN?

Worry is defined in the Merriam-Webster's Collegiate Dictionary as "mental distress or agitation resulting from concern usually for something impending."[438] **Worry** can be **adaptive** in the sense that the individual engages in a process of analyzing the problem, establishing different options, and reacting to the situation accordingly. **Maladaptive worry** refers to the worry that occurs across situations and time, and is both excessive and difficult to control. The research on gender stereotypes has generally concluded that women engage in more worry, both adaptive worry and maladaptive worry, than men, whereas men are more likely to be viewed as engaging in more adaptive than maladaptive worry.[439] This is in line with evidence showing women as more fearful,[440] more insecure,[441] and less agentic.[442] In fact, the research shows that not only people perceive women as experiencing more maladaptive worry than men but also perceive low-status individuals as experiencing more maladaptive worry than high-status individuals. While the research does not examine how this result may influence people's behavior toward women, it does strongly suggest the possibility for serious implications as follows:

> "For example, such a view could influence employers' evaluations of women's

performance or even whether they choose to hire or promote women. It may be the case that employers construe maladaptive worry as affecting the ability to solve problems, and thus they may be hesitant to hire or promote women for positions that require strong problem-solving skills. Indeed, it may be argued that maladaptive worry is related to problem-avoidance and other non constructive problem-solving strategies."[443]

48. IS THE WHITE MALE EFFECT LINKED TO SOCIAL STATUS ANXIETY?

The evidence in the literature is that women worry more than men, and minorities worry more than whites about different risks-from environmental pollution to hand guns, from blood transfusion to red meat.[444] Various explanations have been offered, to include women and minorities' lack of access or understanding of scientific information about risk, lack of empowerment of women and African-Americans, and lack of confidence in the government as compared to white males. These explanations are indeed not convincing. A more convincing explanation emanates from studies that have found that race and sex differences in risk perception can be attributed to a discreet class of high-risk-skeptical white males, who make up around one-third of the white-male population.[445] The phenomenon has been labeled as the **"white male effect"**.[446] Basically, research has shown that white males are less concerned with all manner of risk of global warning, gun accidents, and various medical procedures, than are women and minorities. The research also suggested that these same white males are more likely to hold certain anti-egalitarian and individualistic attitudes than the rest of society.[447] As a result, one study showed that the white male effect is an outgrowth of cultural cognition.[448] In effect, cultural cognition holds that people are motivated by a variety of psychological processes to hold beliefs about putatively dangerous activities that match their cultural evaluation of them. The study, in question, showed that race and gender differences in risk perception are conditional on cultural values. Basically, white males seem to be less concerned about risks only because a discrete group of whites who subscribe to hierarchical and individualistic values are extremely skeptical that activities important to their cultural role and status impose harm on society. This result is supportive of an identity-protective cognition where individual white males selectively credit and dismiss asserted dangers in a manner supportive of their social organization. The white male effect is indeed a reflection of the risk skepticism that hierarchical, and individualistic white males display when activities integral to their cultural identities are challenged as harmful. If an activity is status-enhancing for individuals of a particular cultural persuasion, the same individuals will be motivated by **"status anxiety"** to resist the claim that the activity is dangerous and should be regulated. Of course, they would endorse regulation if the activity is status-diminishing within a cultural group

49. SHOULD YOU BE CAREFUL WITH SOME GIFTS THAT WILL MAKE YOU LOSE SOCIAL STATUS?

There is an informal, mutual insurance mechanism in most gift exchange relationships. As stated a long time ago by a noted anthropologist, "everybody is thereby insured against hunger; he who is in need today receives help from him who may be in like need tomorrow."[449] An increase in wages in a labor contract is really a gift with the expectation of more effort, quality, and attention from the workers.[450] The gift and the counter-gift is the result of self-interest when the giver expects better results from the receiver, or the result of selfishness with foresight. It is not **reciprocal altruism**. There is generally the possibility that the gift exchanges are asymmetrical, as they take place between people endowed with different economic or social status. The nature of the game is therefore to create a situation of subordination when the gift cannot be repaid. Given that the beneficiary is now in a lower rank position vis-à-vis the giver, he or she is likely to experience a feeling of shame for not being able to reciprocate and for finding himself or herself in a lower status position. **Asymmetrical gift exchanges** create social prestige to the donor and social shame to the beneficiary. Stated differently, the person who cannot repay a loan loses his or her rank, and perhaps even his or her status as a free person.[451]

Various studies have examined analytically the relationship between **social prestige** and **social shame** when unequal rank or power positions may get permanently established through asymmetrical gift exchange, and when a gift brings pride and status to the donor and shame to the recipient. The results are as follows:

1. Asymmetrical gift exchange equilibrium can occur only if the importance attached to social shame by a recipient is smaller than that attached to social esteem by a donor. In addition, an income transfer is more likely to be traded against social esteem, status, or power when the weight put on these attempts by the donor or patron is higher.[452]
2. Individuals enjoy the gratitude and sympathy of others if they contribute an above-average effort to the provision of a public good, and a negative approval effect, if their contribution is small.[453]
3. Gift giving is a form of a demand for social approval, and reciprocal gift-giving an instrument in the race for status.[454]
4. **Social exchange theory** led to the hypothesis that status is gained not directly by having the resources, but by using the resources to give gifts. As gifts elicit reciprocity, the failure by the recipient of the gift to reciprocate leads to a subordination of the recipient and more power to the donor.[455] Stated differently, "should another person take a gift and make an equal return, he shows himself to be not only a friend of the given but also his equal

in status. Each party holds the same rank on the dimension of giving and receiving. But what if the other person accepts the gift and does not make a return, he then confesses himself not to be the giver's enemy not his friend but his social inferior."[456]

5. Giving resources to exchange partners that do not reciprocate is sufficient to activate a status element, much like a status characteristic. In other words, given a resource by a donor leads the recipient to offer a positive evaluation of the donor, and a status level, it results in the donor having elevated performance expectations. Similarly, the failure by a low-status individual to reciprocate after a high-status individual gave a gift, leads the high-status individual to negatively evaluate the low-status individual.[457] [458]

50. SHOULD YOU STICK TO THE TOPIC, AND NOT LET OTHERS INTERRUPT OR YOU'LL LOSE STATUS?

The type of language used is a great indicator of the nature and extent of inequality. Getting to express ideas, taking turns at participating, and being less interrupted reflects a higher status position in the group. Various studies examined the relationship between conversational behavior and dominance on one side and **status differentiation**. Some of the findings follow:

1. Conversation analytic researchers showed that high-status people (parents, doctors, men, high power spouses) often enjoy more privileges in conversation than low-status people (children, patients, women, low-power spouses). It seems that status, power, institutional contexts, and local conversational dynamics are more important than social categories in structuring conversational behavior.[459]

2. High-status people are asked their opinions more often, talk more, receive more positive comments, are chosen as leader more frequently, are more likely to influence group decisions, and in general dominate the conversation.[460] Basically, status differentiation not only creates **conversational dominance**, but often legitimizes it.[461]

3. **Interruptions** are a clear violation of turn-taking norms, and are linked to dominance, power, and status. More specifically, high-status people are more likely to interrupt low-status people, with

successful interruptions playing the role of a sensitive measure of actual dominance.[462] Power is more important than gender in determining the use of interruptions in conversation between domestic partners. Men discriminate in their interruption attempts, disrupting the speech of women far more frequently than that of other men, while women do not discriminate, interrupting women and men equally often.[463] It seems that, when it comes to conversational behavior, men are acting as if sex is a status characteristic for both women and men, and in society.[464]

4. When it comes to topic changes, the shifts in conversation seem to be more sensitive to status structures that develop within the conversation rather than to a relatively weak status characteristic like gender.[465] Gender and participation had, however, a subtle effect in the sense that men appear to discriminate and change the subject when it is being developed by women rather than by men, with high-participating speakers often changing the subject developed by lower-participating rather than higher-participating others.

5. Status has implications for the use of language. First, there is evidence of a **linguistic discrimination** resulting from asymmetries of status between minimal groups.[466] Basically, linguistic data were obtained by asking participants to describe a choice (parity vs. ingroup favoritism vs. outgroup favoritism) made by either an in-group or an out-group member in allocating negative

outcomes (i.e., seconds of noise to be listened via earphones). The results showed that high-and-low-status groups described the out-group in a more biased fashion than did equal groups. It is a clear case that asymmetries of status enhance out-group derogation and linguistic discrimination. Second, there is evidence that the **formal versus informal word choices** used in social interaction may serve as a status cue for competence, where formal refers to words used most likely in a textbook, and informal words refer to words used in casual conversation with a friend.[467] Basically, individuals perceive other individuals who use formal words as more competent than those who use informal words.

51. IS THERE MORE ATTITUDINAL AMBIVALENCE FROM THE LOW-STATUS GROUPS?

Both group and system justification motives enter in the decision and/or attitudes of different status groups. Let's examine the meaning and consequences of **group and system justification**, how they may end up in conflict, and how is this conflict resolved?

Group justification is mainly manifest in **ingroup favoritism**. By favoritism, it is meant the situation where a person favors another person, not because he/she is doing the best job, but rather because of some extraneous features-membership in a favored group, personal likes, and dislikes, especially, but not limited to, in cases of hiring, honoring, or awarding contracts.[468] It is one of the most important sources of workplace conflict and stress. Politics and power struggles within organizations may result in favoritism, and also can cause favoritism.Favoritism, and especially **in-group favoritism**, manifests itself differently among different status groups. Basically, there is the assumption that members of disadvantaged groups could not help but internalize society's biases against them, and to adopt certain preferences for other, more advantaged groups.[469] It is a kind of inferiority complex of identifying with the aggressor, followed by resentment against one's own kind, who is, however unintentionally, the reason for one's suffering.[470] It is a kind of **self-hatred** that encumbered minority groups low in social status.[471] The Marxist theorists saw the phenomenon in terms of **dominant ideology, cultural hegemony, and false consciousness**, and describe it as the internalization by members of the disadvantaged groups of the cultural values and stereotypes of the very social system that oppresses them.[472] It is best evident by findings indicating strong evidence of **outgroup favoritism** among members of groups that are assigned the position of low status.[473] The outgroup favoritism by low-status groups, a form of acceptance of their own inferiority, is only present on dimensions that are highly relevant to the status differences.[474] They will show more ingroup favoritism on irrelevant dimensions as a way of compensating for an otherwise negative social identity, and as a way of alleging their superiority on irrelevant dimensions.

System justification arises from a socially acquired motive to justify and rationalize the existing social system on bases that include stereotyping, ideology, deservingness, desirability, and even memory.[475] System justification works differently among different status groups with different social psychological effects. While for members of high status groups, system justification is generally associated with ingroup favoritism, increased self-esteem, and decreased ambivalence, depression, and neuroticism, for members of low-status groups, it is associated with outgroup favoritism, ingroup ambivalence, decreased self-esteem, increased depression, and increased neuroticism.[476] This shows that there is a serious conflict between group and system justification for both status groups. The problem is to determine which status group experiences the most attitudinal ambivalence? There is evidence that disadvantaged group members experience a high degree of ambivalence with regards to social identification, with the example of African American children expressing ambivalent attitudes about black dolls, and experiencing some degree of confusion around issues of racial self-identification.[477] Similarly, high-status groups hold ambivalent attitudes towards low-status groups, such as women,[478] and then physically disabled.[479] When combining both group and system justification, the findings show that among members of psychologically meaningful groups that are low in status, ambivalence toward the ingroup intensifies as system justification motives are increased.[480] Similarly, for members that are high in social status groups, ambivalence is negatively related to system justification, insofar as group justification and system justification motives are complimentary for high-status groups. It shows that perception of legitimacy increases ingroup favoritism and decreases ingroup ambivalence among members of high status groups but decreases ingroup favoritism, and increases ingroup ambivalence among members of low-status groups. In short, there is more attitudinal ambivalence among the low-status groups.

To conclude, given the known arguments that people have strong motives to (a) legitimize the self, (b) legitimize the group, and (c) legitimize the system, the results indicating that for members of low-status groups, these motives are often in conflict or contradiction, resulting in ambivalence, and adds to the results that the same groups experience **decreased ideological coherence,**[481] **disengagement from the system,**[482] **partial or total dis-identification with the ingroup,**[483] **and individual mobility and group exit**[484]**.**

52. IS YOUR SOCIAL STATUS AFFECTING YOUR HEALTH?

When it comes to the relationship between social status and health, two hypotheses have been used. One called the "**social causation**" hypothesis argues that socioeconomic status affects health through mechanisms that are not entirely understood. The other hypothesis called the "**health selection**" or the "**drift**" hypothesis argues that an individual's health influences their ability to attain or maintain desirable socioeconomic positions and resources. Although the results regarding the relative merit of the social causation and health selection hypotheses is mixed, the concern in this book is with the consequences of status. The social causation hypothesis, with the notion that status determines wealth, is the issue. The findings on the social causation hypothesis are interesting and should be the basis for health policies at the local and national levels. Two important findings are that:

a) those at the bottom of the socioeconomic scale have worse health than those above them in the hierarchy, and,

b) there is a social gradient in health in individuals who are not poor. The higher the social position a person has, the better his/her health will be. This second finding has been labeled the **status syndrome**.[485] Evidence on the status syndrome and the **social gradient in health** and the impact of status on health follows:

1. The phenomenon of the social gradient in coronary heart disease (CHD) was first noted in the **Whitehall study** of British Civil Servants.[486] While CHD was commonly viewed as a disease of affluence caused by stress and affluent lifestyle, the Whitehall study showed that the individuals second from the top of the occupational hierarchy had higher CHD mortality rates than those above them, and those third from the top had higher rates still.

2. Status may be early life status (e.g. parental schooling), ascribed social status (e.g. sex, race, ethnicity), and achieved social status (e.g. schooling, economic resources). There is ample evidence documenting that higher achieved status lead to access to and better health, and play an important role in understanding inequalities in health.[487] An examination of the relative impact of early life status, ascribed status, and achieved status on behavioral health risks (e.g. weight, smoking, drinking, physical activity) found that early life, achieved and ascribed social statuses strongly predict behavioral health risks, although the effects are stronger in midlife than in old age.[488]

3. Social status most likely will help you live longer. Think of Nobel Prize winners as individuals that found higher status suddenly dropped on them. In fact, a study of Nobel prize winners in physics

and chemistry between 1901 and 1950 found that a) the prize winners lives 1.4 years longer on average-or 77.2 years-than those who were nominated for the award, and b) when just comparing the Nobel winners and nominees from the same country, the longevity gap widened about 8 months on average.[489] It was a clear evidence of a case where social status affects lifespan and confers **"health-giving magic".**

4. Losing social status and sliding down the social ladder can have an impact on the health of those affected. What would be the reaction of males and females who experience such a downward social shift? It seems that men who lose status during their lifetime take the blow much harder than women in the same position as they are more likely to suffer depression than women.[490] What's even more interesting is the fact that women are twice as likely to slide down the social ladder and yet avoid the depression and poor psychological wellbeing experienced by men in the same position. Losing social status affects the mental health of both women and men, with men suffering more.

5. The **inverse gradient** between social status and health was generally confirmed with measure of objective status. The question is whether or not subjective social status is a good predictor of health and change in health status? It appears that both subjective and objective social status measures are able to predict health. There are,

however, some interesting findings about subjective social status as follows:

A. Women's ladder ranking was a stronger predictor of health-related factors (psychological functioning, self-rated health, heart rate, sleep, body mass index, and cortisol habituation to repeated stress) than was objective social status.[491]

B. Subjective status is a better predictor of health status and decline in health status over time in middle-aged adults, showing subjective status as a more precise measure of social position.[492]

C. In a telephone survey of Canadian adults, perceived social position relative to all Canadians appeared to be a strong predictor of self-rated health.[493]

D. In a study of older persons in Hong Kong, it appears that somatic complaints, physical disease, and functional and mental health status were related to self-rated economic conditions. with the relationships being stronger for mental health compared to physical health.[494]

E. In a population representative sample of elderly and nearly elderly men and women in Taiwan, low ladder ranking was associated with poor health outcomes with stronger effects for those who had six or fewer years of education compared to those with more education.[495]

F. Among young pregnant women who quit smoking because of pregnancy, low subjective social status was associated with a constellation of characteristics indicative of increased vulnerability to postpartum smoking, with subjective social status providing unique information on risk for postpartum smoking over and above the effects of race/ethnicity, objective socioeconomic status, and partner status.[496]

These inequities in health are present in both developed and developing countries, begging for an answer to the question why there is a social gradient in health. The fact is that the social gradient in health is not due to differences in medical care, or primarily to differences in health behavior, or to differences in natural circumstances.[497] It is strictly related to status. Differences in social status imply differences in control and in social participation, which are both widely viewed as important to better access to health care and hence contribute to inequities in health. Low participation in social networks is linked to increased risk of a range of diseases,[498] and increased mortality rates.[499] Similarly, low control at work was linked to low heart rate variability.[500]

53. IS AGING LINKED TO SOCIAL STATUS?

Not only does status affect health and age-related disease, it appears to have an impact on the aging process itself. **Telomeres** are key pieces of DNA thought to correlate to biological age. Basically, they are repeat sequences of DNA that sit on the ends of chromosomes, protecting them from damage. With the passing of time and people aging, the telomeres become shorter and shorter, exposing the cells to damage and death. A study published in 2006 examined the white blood cells of 1,552 female twins and produced two interesting findings as follows:[501]

1. After adjusting the factors that influence aging like obesity, smoking and lack of exercise, it appeared that telomeres in women placed in lower social status were significantly shorter, and more likely to die prematurely and die from early cardiovascular diseases and cancer. They were in terms of cellular age, seven years "older".

2. Examining the telomeres length of 17 pairs of twins, who started life in the same social status but married in different social status groups, it appears in 12 cases that the telomeres of the twins in the high social status group were significantly longer than those in the lower social status group: the difference equated to about nine biological years.

Being in a lower social status seems to create the kind of stress that accelerates aging, and may explain the differences sometimes observed between chronological and biological ages.

54. DOES SOCIAL STATUS LEAD TO DOMINANCE AND CONFLICT?

Status-and group-based social hierarchies are due to one characteristic that an individual or group possesses that gives them more power and privilege, and to a heightened sense of entitlement to society's resources, including health care, education and attractive employment. These characteristics, used to determine status and group-based social hierarchies, come in different forms depending on the context and are not limited to race, ethnicity, gender, age, skin color, economic class, caste, religious sect, and regional grouping.[502] The status and group-based social hierarchies are a basis for social stratification and a basis of inequality as some are favored over the others for a lot of privileges.[503] Needless to say, some may resist leading to social conflicts between those perceiving themselves at the top of the social, economic, and/or political hierarchy and those at the bottom of the same hierarchy. There is evidently a situation of domination leading to both group conflict and even oppression, as once group gains dominance, it generally monopolizes resources in order to maintain and perpetuate its privilege status. One may view most cases of group conflict and oppression (e. g. **racism, ethnocentrism, sexism, nationalism, and regionalism**) as a direct result of the drive for status and the formation of group-based social hierarchies. Each of these hierarchies create opposing groups with one group feeling threatened and oppressed, and may be tempted to defend itself by retaliating, and another group attempting through various means to maintain and perpetuate its privileges. Status implies a dominant group and another deferring to it, as well as a group, implicitly accepting the inequality, especially if the inequality is built through the social system itself using various forms of structural components and institutions.[504]

55. WHAT HAPPENS IF AN INDIVIDUAL RATES DIFFERENTLY ON DIFFERENT TYPES OF STATUS?

Social status may be conceptualized as a composite of multiple vertical dimensions, some of which can be viewed as investments in a social situation while others are viewed as rewards arising from that situation. The investments are either achieved investments such as education, or ascribed investments such as ethnicity. The rewards are either social rewards such as occupational quality or material rewards such as income. If the various dimensions of status are not in conflict or contradiction, there is **status consistency** or **status crystallization**: a form of **status coherence**. **Status inconsistency** arises when an individual's social positions on the dimensions and the rewards are both positive and negative. The theory posits that individuals who are inconsistent among these dimensions and rewards are more likely to have different attitudes and behaviors than those who are consistent.[505] [506] A state of **distributive justice** exists when individuals who are high on education and/or ethnicity are receiving greater rewards in terms of occupational quality and income. In effect, it is suggested that the balance of investments (e.g. education) versus rewards (e.g. income) is at the heart of actual effects of apparent status inconsistency.[507] Where the investments are higher than the rewards, individuals will experience injustice and feel anger. In addition, a conflict will be created as these individuals will like to emphasize their higher rank while the rest of society may focus on the lower rank. These individuals will most likely blame society for a failure in maintaining distributive justice, and will act and/or behave in ways aimed at reestablishing equity. Basically, individuals hold cognitive beliefs about the proper relationship between their investments and the rewards they are receiving. Any imbalance between the two leads to frustration and an experience of **cognitive dissonance.** Reducing the dissonance may take place in different ways:

1. They may try to improve the ranking on one or more of the dimensions of status;
2. They are likely to develop a more liberal political outlook; rich Jews voting as liberals is a good example.
3. They may resort to various forms of social isolation, from withdrawal to suicide;
4. They may join whatever ideology that may lead to social change;
5. They may experience high rates of psychomatic symptoms;
6. They may resort to prejudice as a result of increased competition, and to superiority by a perceived ethnic subordinate.[508]

56. WHAT'S THE SITUATION FOR LOW STATUS PEOPLE? (THE GOOD, THE BAD, AND THE UGLY).

The classification of individuals as low-status individuals is rationalized by one of the most influential school of sociology in the United States-**the structural-functionalist perspective**- which views the **status-role unit** as the basic element of social stratification.[509] As a result they are ranked in terms of lesser privileges and prestige.

There are specific instances where low-status may be preferred:

1. An individual may prefer to hold a lower status job in a firm, just to be able to be associated with higher-quality co-workers that are able to raise the status of the firm. This has been refereed to as the **"halo effect"** or the chance to be part of **"status group"**.[510]

2. An individual may prefer to keep a low status job, if the higher status job or situation implies a "ceiling" has been reached and no future promotions or wage increases are expected. This has been referred to as the **"dead-end effect"**.[511]

3. An individual may prefer to stay with a lower status job in a top-quality situation, if it could lead him or her to learn from the high quality co-workers. This has been referred to as the **"learning effect"**.[512]

In fact, the whole status process depends on the low status members. Basically, status is gained and maintained when the other members of the group-the low status members- are complicit rather than coerced, with compliance involving not only initial acceptance but also internalization to insure lasting effects.[513] In fact, the degree of status diffusion is best expressed by two extremes. At one extreme, an individual's status is just the sum of the deference acts shown by his or her immediate contacts. At the other extreme, the individual's status is the result of not only the deference shown by his or her contacts, but also the status of the contacts. Baron de Rothschild, when asked by a friend for a loan, replied "I won't give a loan myself; but I will walk arm-in-arm with you across the floor of the Stock exchange, and you soon shall have willing lenders to spare."

The individuals assigned to the low-status condition are far from receiving a fair treatment. In effect, the favorable treatment given to a person of high social status is likely to take various forms: transfer of market goods, transfer of non-market goods (e.g., through marriage), transfer of authority (letting the high status person be the leader), modified behavior (such as deference or cooperation), and symbolic acts (such as showing respect).[514]

Social status may have a functional role by serving the collective interests of privilege groups who use it as an instrument to restrict entry and improve modes of behavior. To join the privileged status group, potential members have to emerge in costly conspicuous consumption or avoid gainful work **(noblesse oblige)**, both of which cause the equilibrium to be socially inefficient.[515]

Low-status people may strive to upgrade their status level. The upgrading can be attained by three ways: by birth, by earnings status, and by association. Status can be acquired by association with high status individuals, hoping that by associating themselves with a successful person or team, others will be motivated to treat them in a positive fashion.[516]

The status of an actor is generally assumed to be strongly correlated with an actor's quality where quality refers to the actor's potential and desire to contribute to the group. If the correlation is not perfect, the conclusion is that there is a strong **social construction** in the group, and therefore, there is a need to decouple an actor's status from an actor's underlying quality.[517]

It is a vicious cycle as low status members who attempt to gain status in a group by actively contributing to the group task often draw a negative reaction from other group members. Their assertive contribution is seen as illegitimate and subject to others' sanctions. The reason is that a legitimacy process may have developed in which group members socially construct a normative "right" to earn status for those associated with the high state of the status characteristic.[518]

People react differently to others in their status group, to individuals in other groups (out-groups), because people attach a positive value to being able to differentiate themselves from others, especially in a positive light.[519] In fact, conferring status on a group legitimizes its members' superiority and makes them feel that they deserve, and thus work to obtain, better outcomes for members of their own group.[520] Status is different, however, from favor since it was shown that higher status increases the tendency to reward one's own group, whereas increased favor reduces the tendency to reward one's own group.[521] It is only status that reinforces the tendency to reward members of one's own group. The research goes further by showing that high-status individuals discriminate in favor of equal-status individuals and against lower-status individuals.[522]

It is still a fact that the dichotomy between high-status and low-status level is a zero sum game where the gain by the high-status Individual is matched by a loss incurred by the low-status individual; and it is impossible to raise every body's status. This confirm the view of status as "an inferiority-superiority scale with respect to the comparative degree to which [actors] possess or embody some socially-approved or generally desired attribute or characteristic."[523] In addition, the effects of upgrade in status are positive while the effects of downgrade in status are strictly negative.

High-status raises an individual's power and may lead to lower status individuals unconsciously burying their will to resist. This was shown in a study in which "experimenters [drove] either a flashy new Chrysler or a beat-up old Ford to a stop light and [remained] there after the light had turned green."[524] The results of the experiment showed that 84% of the drivers behind the Ford honked their horns while only 50% of those behind the Chrysler did so, and that two of the former actually hit the experimental car. In addition, a study found consistently higher rate and blood pressure readings among subjects interacting with individuals who outranked them than found among subjects interacting with individuals of equal rank.[525]

Low-status individuals, or non-elites, are sometimes convinced to maintain the status quo, when they are reminded by the high-status individuals, or **elites**, that their situation is much better than an **"outcast"** group. It is justly observed that "outcasts are a reminder to nonelites that their situation could be much worse; the recurring dilemma for respectable nonelites is whether their antipathies are best directed at elites or at outcasts."[526]

It may be that people have rationalized the need for low-status groups.For example, individuals have a positive bias towards persons with high-status. This may be the result of the **"just-world" theory** that suggests that many people believe that in a just world people get what they deserve and deserve what they get.[527] It also follows from the ample evidence that individuals discriminate in favor of others with equal or higher status and against those of lower status.[528] The situation is aggravated by the findings that the suggestions of high-status individuals are generally accepted in disproportionate numbers, even if in correct;

and the suggestions of low-status individuals are rejected in disproportionate number, even if correct.[529] Needless to say, the low status individuals live in a constant **status panic** over their inferior position in contemporary society, creating conflicts between status groups, referred to as **"the politics of resentment".**

One way for low-status individuals to 'ape" the high-status individuals is to adopt their way of speaking. One example is the recent popularity of the word "curate". Once rarely spoken outside museums, it is now pasted onto any activity that involves willing and selecting.[530] It is a way of implying that there is a similarity between what a low-status individual does and what someone with an advanced degree does. It is a blatant adoption of the vernacular of prestigious professions by members of less pedigreed professions.

57. DOES SOCIAL STATUS AFFECT THE WORKING OF FIRMS, SOCIETY, AND THE ECONOMY?

There are definite connections between social status and the workings of firms and the economy. Separate individuals with their own self-interest make a firm. Simply assuming individuals' behavior is strictly influenced only by a maximization of consumption and wealth is clearly an unreasonable assumption. That explains the accepted inclusion of a more general social behavior, such as altruism, emotionally- driven social exchange, and the quest for status in discourses about the workings of firms and the economy. Examples follow:

1. Status has a definite impact on employment. There is a definite correlation between attending a high-status university and job success.[531] When using for help a contact person who works for a firm, the higher the status of the contact person, the better one's employment outcome will be in terms of occupational prestige.[532]

2. CEO's compensation is also determined and negotiated with a compensation committee. Status plays a role, given that when a CEO holds higher status than the chair of the compensation committee, he or she will receive higher than the average pay.[533]

3. There are consequences to workers worrying about status when applying for jobs. For one thing, it was argued that unemployed people, unlike immigrants, are often reluctant to accept

temporary but low-paid jobs because that would imply a loss of status.[534] Similarly, within firms, productivity differentials may exceed wage differentials when a reward is derived from higher status.[535]

4. Given that there are three broad incentives that govern the behavior of individuals in society: a) private rewards such as wages and profits, b) social rewards such as prestige and status, and c) rules and laws that enforce certain types of behavior and penalize deviations, the question is under which circumstances the social rewards will provide an effective and feasible mechanism that may replace laws and rules? One answer is provided by the suggestion that social rewards, such as status, which are relatively cheap, can be used to regulate externalities if the socially-minded individuals who care about social status will not be driven away by asocial individuals who selfishly maximize their fitness.[536] This is possible only in a society in which individuals who care about their standing in society can survive in the long run.[537]

5. When externalities or higher transaction costs cause markets to fail to exist or to perform efficiently, social rewards through the assignment of higher status to individuals may be used to regulate trading activities. For example, in the case of basic reward, the innovator may be willing to ignore the free ride by other individuals, and the absence of compensation if he or she is given recognition and esteem, making status a signal which will be privately and socially useful.[538]

6. Consumer behavior and the general health of the economy change every now and them as a result of economic crises. There are two related research results. First, status becomes associated with more work-related products than in the past.[539] Second, in an economic downturn, consumers may shy away from paying an additional amount for the increased value of status, while in an economic recovery they may revert again to buying status.[540] As Kayne West rapped, **"I as Kom the Louis Vuitton Don-Bought my mom a purse, now she is Louis Vuitton mom."**

7. In examining the impact of social status on the market, it appears that status has a significant impact on prices and earnings. More specifically the average prices are higher in markets where higher-status sellers face lower-status buyers, and lower when buyers have higher status than sellers.[541] In addition, the high-status side of the market captures a greater share of surplus earnings significantly more than their lower-status counterparts. This implies that people are willing to pay higher prices to acquire higher status. As stated by the authors:

> "In today's markets, it explains why products associated with holding high statuscommand a premium over other items. The value of status drives the advertising industry to employ celebrity endorsements, so that consumers will perceive a good as a signal for higher status. It causes the same house to command a higher price in a high-status

neighborhood, workers to forgo earnings for rank in the workplace, and ordinary citizens to pay high prices for items that once belonged to celebrities."[542]

8. In exploring the economic basis for the value of status by creating status in an experiment, one study showed that status affects the behavior of individuals in the sense that high-status individuals are treated favorably relative to low-status individuals.[543] To explore this result and the light it sheds on consumers' concern with status in their decisions to purchase goods and services, another experiment by the same authors concluded that buying status is rational because high status favorably affects one's outcome in economic situations.[544] Witness the following observation: "The way we dress reflects not only our personality but also our economic, political, and social standing and our own self worth. Luxury adornment has always been at the top of the pyramid, setting the haves from the have-nots. Its defining elements-silk, gold and silver, precious and semi-precious stones, fur-have been culturally recognized and sought after the millennia."[545]

9. Various studies examined the possible trade-offs between status, earnings and economic efficiency. Examples follow:

a. One study investigated the implications for risk-taking behavior if individuals care about their own wealth and about the status induced by having high wealth relative to the rest of the population.[546]

b. On study explored the welfare-reducing potential of the rat-race pursuit of relative income.[547]

c. One study constructed a general equilibrium model where status and wages are endogenously determined.[548]

d. One study models status seeking as a game where one player's success in achieving status reduces other players' returns from status and showed the quest for status can lead to economic efficiency.[549]

In general, the research on status that modeled the economic implications of the desire to win the status contest, concluded that status seeking behavior diverts resources from productive use, and is welfare-reducing relative to the outcome where individuals do not engage in this behavior.

ENDNOTES

1 Warner, W. Lloyd, meeker, Marchia, and Eells, Kenneth, *Social Class in America*, New York: Harper and Row, 1960, p. 10.

2 Weber, Max, *Economy and Society*, Berkeley: University of California press, 1978, p. 305.

3 Ball, Sheyl B., Eckel, Catherine C., Grossman, Philip J., and Zame, William, "Status in markets," *Quarterly Journal of Economics*, 116, 1, 2001, p. 161.

4 Abercombie, N., Hill, S., , and Turner,B. S., *Sovereign Individuals of Capitalism*, London: Allen and Unwin, 1984.

5 Frank, R. H., *Passions within reason: The strategic role of the emotions*. NY: Norton, 1988, p. 53.

6 Berger, peter L., *Invitation to Sociology: A Humanistic Perspective*, garden City, NY: Doubleday and Company, 1963, p. 133.

7 Marshall. T., *Class Citizenship and Social Development: Essays*, Chicago: University of Chicago Press, 1977, p. 198.

8 Hirschman, A., "An alternative explanation of Contemporary harried ness," *Quarterly Journal of Economics*, 87, 4, p. 634.

9 Weber, M., *The protestant Ethic and the Spirit of Capitalism*, NY, NY: Scribner's, 1958.

10 Henrich, Joseph, and Gil-White, Francisco J., "The evolution of prestige: freely conferred deference as a mechanism for enhancing the benefits of cultural transmission," *Evolution and Human behavior*, 22, 2001, p. 165.

11 Weisfeld, G. E., and Beresford, J. M., "Erectness of posture as an indicator of dominance or success in humans," *Motivation and Emotion*, 6, 1982, pp. 113-131.

12 Berger, J., Fisek, M. H., Norman, R. Z., and Wagner, D. C., "The formation of reward expectations in status situation," In Messick, D. M., and Cook, K., (Ed.), *Equity Theory:*

Psychological and Sociological Perspectives, NY: Praeger, 1987, p. 131.

13 Troyer, Lisa, and Younts, C. Wesley, "Whose expectations matter? The relative power of first- and second-order expectations in determining social influence," *American Journal of Sociology*, CIII, 1997, pp. 692-732.

14 Berger, Joseph, Rosenholtz, Susan J., and Zelditch, Morris, "Status organizing processes," *Annual Review of Sociology*, 6, 1980, pp. 479-508.

15 Moore, James C., "Status and influence in small group interactions," *Sociometry*, 31, 1968, pp. 47-63.

16 Berger, Joseph, Cohen, Bernard P., and Zelditch, Morris, "Status characteristics and social interaction," *American Sociological Review*, 37, 1972, pp. 241-255.

17 Bourdieu, P., *Distinctions, A Social Critique of the Judgment of Taste*, London and New York: Routledge and Kegan Paul, 1986.

18 Anderson, Cameron, John, Oliver, P., Keltner, Dacher, and Kring, Ann M., "Who attains social status? Effects of personality and physical attractiveness in social groups," *Journal of Personality and Social Psychology*, 1, 81, 2001, p.116.

19 Fiske, S.T., "Controlling other people: The impact of power on stereotyping," *American Psychologist*, 48, 1993, pp. 621-628.

20 Goldhamer, H., and Shils, E. A., "Types of power and status," *American Journal of Sociology*, 45, 1939, pp. 171-182.

21 Berger, J., Cohen, B. P., and Zelditch, M., "Status characteristics and social interaction," *American Sociological Review*, 37, 1972, pp. 241-255.

22 Hogan, R., Curphy, G.J., and Hogan, J., "What we know about leadership: Effectiveness and personality," *American Psychologist*, 49, 1994, pp. 493-504.

23 Raven, B.H., and French, J.R.P., Jr, "Group support, legitimate power, and social influence", *Journal of Personality*, 26, 1958, pp. 402-409.

24 *The Wall Street Journal*, :What Managers Really Do", Monday August 17, 2009, p.R2

25 Emerson, R.M., "Over-dependence relations" Op. Cit, pp. 31-41

26 Willer, David, and Anderson, Bo, (Eds.). *Networks, Exchange, and Coercion* New York: Elsevier, 1981.

27 Kipnis, D. *The Powerholders*. Chicago: The University of Chicago Press, 1976.

28 Kipnis, D, Castell, J., Gergen, M., and Mauch, D., "Metamorphic effects of power," *Journal of Applied Psychology*, 2, 61, 1976, pp. 127-135.

29 Benoit-Smullyan, Emile, "Status, status types, and status interrelations," *American Sociological Review*, 9, 1944, p. 159.

30 Keize, Izuma, Daisuke, N. Saito, and Norihiro Sadato, "Processing of Social and Monetary rewards in the human striatum", *Neuron*, 58, 2, 2008, pp. 284-294.

31 Zink, Caroline F., Tong, Yunscia, Chen, Qiang, and Myer-Linderberg, Andreas, "Know your place: Neural processing of social hierarchy in humans," *Neuron*, 58, 2, 2008, pp. 273-283.

32 Schwarz, Alan, "' The greatest': What a concept," *The New York Times*, June 14, 2009.

33 Adler, N.E., Epel, E., Castellazo, G., and Ickovics, "Relationship of subjective and objective social status with psychological and physiological functioning: Preliminary data in healthy white women, *Health Psychology*, 1, 2000, pp. 586-592.

34 Judge, C. M., James-Hawkins, L., Yzerbyt, V., and Kashima, Y., "Fundamental dimensions of social judgment: Understanding the relations between judgments of competence and warmth, *Journal of Applied Psychology*, 89, 2004, pp.428-441.

35 Berger, J., Fisek, M. H., Norman, R.Z., and Zelditch, M., *Status characteristics and social interaction: An expectation-states approach*. New York: Elsevier, 1977.

36 Berger, J., Rosenholtz, S.J., and Zelditch, M., "Status organizing processes, *Annual Review of Sociology*, 6, 1980, pp. 479-508.
37 Fiske, S. E., Cuddy, A., C., Glick, P., and Xu, J., "A model of (often mixed) stereotype content: Competence and warmth respectively follow from perceived status and competition," *Journal of Personality and Social Psychology*, 82, 2002, pp. 878-902.
38 Conway, M., Pizzamiglio, M.T., and Mount, L., "Status, communality, and agency: Implications for stereotypes of gender and other groups." *Journal of Personality and Social Psychology*, 71, 1996, pp. 25-38.
39 Webster, M., Jr., and driskell, J. E., "status generalization: A review and some data," *American Sociological Review*, 43, 1978, pp. 220-236.
40 Fiske, S. E., Xu, J., Cuddy, A. C., and Glick, P., "(dis) respecting versus (dis)liking: Status and interdependence predict ambivalent stereotypes of competence and warmth," *Journal of Social issues*, 55, 1999, pp. 473-489.
41 Knottnerus, J., D., "Social structural analysis and status generalization: the contribution and potential of expectation states theory," In Szmatka, J., Skvoretz, I., and berger, J. (Eds.), *Status, networks, and Structure*, Stanford, CA: Stanford University press, 1997, p. 126.
42 Fragale, A. R., Rosen, B., Xu, C., and Onypchnk, I., "The higher they are, the harder they fall: The effects of wrongdoer status on observer punishment, recommendations and intentionality attributions," *Organizational behavior and Human decision Processes,* 2009.
43 Ibid.
44 Carli, L.L., and Eagly, A. H., "Gender effects on social influence and emerging leadership". In Powell, G., N., (Ed.), *Handbook of Gender and Work*. Thousands Oaks, CA: Sage. Pp. 203-222.
45 Humphrey, R., "How work roles influence perception: Structural cognitive processes and organizational

behavior, "American *Sociological Review*, 50, 1985, pp.242-252.

46 Sande, G. N., Ellard, J. H., and Ross, M., "Effect of arbitrary assigned status labels on self-perceptions and social perceptions: The mere position effect," *Journal of Personality and Social Psychology*, 50, 1986, pp. 684-689.

47 Foschi, M., "Double standards for competence: theory and research," *Annual Review of Sociology*, 26, 2000, pp. 21-42.

48 Depret, E., and Fiske, S./T., "Social cognition and power: Some cognitive consequences of social structure as a source of control deprivation." In Weary, G., Gleicher, F., and Marsh, K. L., (Eds.), *Control Motivation and Social Cognition*. New York: Springer-Verlag, 1993, pp. 176-202.

49 Ng, S. K., *The Social Psychology of Power*. New York: Academic press. 1980.

50 Ridgeway, C. L., and Blackwell, J. W., "Group processes and the diffusion of status beliefs," *Social Psychology Quarterly*, 60, 1997, pp. 14-31.

51 Raven, B. H., and Kruglanski, A., W., "Conflict and power," In Swingle, P. G.,(Ed.), *The Structure of Conflict*, New York, Academic Press, pp. 69-110.

52 Berger, J., Wagner, D. G., and Zelditch, M., *Introduction: Expectations states theory: Review and Assessment. Status, Rewards, and influence: How Expectations Organize Behaviour*. San Francisco: Jossey-Bass, 1985. pp. 1-72.

53 Ball, S. B/, and Eckel, C., C., "Buying status: Experimental evidence on status in negotiations," *Psychology and Marketing*, 13, 1996, pp. 381-405.

54 Ball, S. B., Eckel, C. C., Grossman, P. J., and Zame, W., "Status in Markets," *Quarterly Journal of Economics*, 116, 2001, pp. 161-188.

55 Ridgeway, C. L., Boyle, E. H., Knipers, K. J., and Robinson, D. T., "How do status beliefs develop? The role of resources

and international experience," *American Sociological Review*, 63, 1998, pp. 331-350.

56 Fershtman, Chaim, Hvide, hans K., and Weiss, Yoram, "Cultural diversity, status concerns and the organization of work," *Working Paper* Tel Aviv university, 2005.

57 Tajfel, H., and Turner, J. C., "The social identity of intergroup behaviour," In Worchel, S., and Austin, W. G. (Eds.), *Psychology of Intergroup Relations*. Chicago: nelson-Hall, 1986.

58 Sachdev, I., and Bourbis, R. Y., "Status differential and intergroup behavior," *European Journal of Social Psychology*, 17, 1987, pp. 277-294.

59 Ellemers, Naomi, Doosje, Bert J., Van Knippenberg, N., and Wilke, hence, "Status protection in high status minority groups," *European Journal of Social Psychology*, 2, 22, 1992, pp. 123-140.

60 Blau, peter M., "Social mobility and interpersonal relationships," *American Sociological Review*, 21, 3, 1956, pp. 290-295.

61 Aronson, E., and Bridgeman, D., "Jigsaw groups and the desegregated classroom: In pursuit of common goals," *personality and Social Psychology Bulletin*, 5, 4, 1979, pp. 438-446.

62 Cooke, K., "Expectations, evaluations and equity," *American Sociological Review*, 40, 1973, pp. 372-388.

63 Pfeffer, J., "Organizational demography," in Staw, B., and Cummings, L., (Eds.), *Research in Organizational Behavior*. Greenwich, CT: JAI Press, 5, 1983, pp. 299-357.

64 Turner, J. C., and brown, R. J., "Status, position, and legitimacy in the minimal group paradigm," In Tajfel, H. (Ed.), *Differentiation between Social Groups: Studies in the Social Psychology of Intergroup Relations*. London: Academic Press, Inc, 1978.

65 Park, Robert E., *Human Communities*. New York: The Free Press, 1952.

66 Cunneff, Tom, "insider," *People Magazine*, 59, 2003, p. 55.
67 Ridgeway, C., *The Dynamics of Small Groups*, NY: St. Martin's, 1983, p. 160.
68 Shils, Edward A., "Deference" In Jackson, John, (Ed.), *Social Stratification*, Cambridge University Press, 1968, pp. 104-29.
69 York, Erin and Cornwell, Benjamin, "Status on trial: Social characteristics and influence in the jury room," *Social Forces*, 1, 85, 2008, p. 457.
70 Colwell, Brian, "Deference or respect? Status management practices among prison inmates,: *Social Psychology Quarterly*, 4, 70, 2007, pp. 442-443.
71 Goffman, Erving, "The nature of deference and demeanor," *American Anthropologist*, 58, 1956, pp. 473-502.
72 Collins, Randall, and Arnett, john, "A short history of deference and demeanor," In Collins, Randall, *Conflict Sociology: Toward an Explanatory Science*, Academic press, NY, 1975, pp. 161-224.
73 Emerson, Richard, "Exchange theory, part II: Exchange relations and networks," In Berger, J., Zelditch Sr., M., and Anderson, B., (Eds.), *Sociological Theories in Progress*, Vol 2. Boston, MA: Houghton Mifflin, 1972, pp. 58-87.
74 McElroy, J., and Morrow, P., "personal space, personal appearance and personal selling, "Psychological *Reports*, 74, 1994, pp. 425-426.
75 Goodman, M., and Gareis, C., "The influence of status on decisions to help," *The Journal of Social Psychology*, 133, 1993, pp. 23-31.
76 Gueguen, Nicolas, and Pichot, Nathalie, "The influence of status on pedestrians' failure to observe a road-safety rule," *The Journal of Social Psychology*, June 2001.
77 Cohen, Joel E., *Casual Groups of Monkeys and Men; Stochastic Models of Elementary Social Systems*. Cambridge, MA: Harvard University press, 1990.

78 Bourgeois, Philippe I., *In Search of Respect: Selling Crack in El Barrio*. New York, NY: Cambridge University press, 2003.
79 Morrill, Calvin, *The Executive Way: Conflict Management in Corporations*, Chicago: University of Chicago Press, 1995.
80 Goodman, M., and Gareis, C., "the influence of status on decision to help," *The Journal of Social Psychology*, 141, 2001, pp. 413-415.
81 Greegen, Nicholas, and Alexander, Pascual, "Status and people's tolerance toward ill-mannered person: A field study," *Journal of Mundane Behavior*, May 2003, pp. 29-36.
82 Kleinke, C., "Effects of dress on compliance to requests in a field setting," *The Journal of Social Psychology*, 101, 1977, pp. 223-224.
83 McElroy, J., and Morrow, P., "Personal space, personal appearance, and personal selling," *Psychological Reports*, 74, 1994, pp. 425-426.
84 Bickman, L., "The effects of social status on the honesty of others," *The Journal of Social Psychology*, 85, 1971, pp. 87-92.
85 Solomon, H., and Herman, L., "Status symbols and prosocial behavior: The effect of the victim's car on helping," *The Journal of Psychology*, 97, 1977, pp. 271-223.
86 Fornbrum, Charles, J., "Corporate reputation as economic assets," In Hitt, M. A., Freeman, R. E., and Harrison, J. S., (Eds.), *The Blackwell Handbook of Strategic Management*, Oxford: Blackwell Publishers, Ltd., 2001.
87 Thyre, S. R., "A status value theory of power in exchange relations," *American Sociological Review*, 65, 2000, pp. 407-432.
88 Ridgeway, C., and Dickema, D., "Dominance and collective hierarchy formation in male and female task groups," *American Sociological Review*, 54, 1989, pp. 79-93.

89 Dovidio, J. F., and Ellyson, S., L., "Decoding visual dominance: Attributions of power based on relative percentage of looking while speaking and looking while listening," *Social Psychology Quarterly*, 45, 1982, pp. 106-113.
90 Fiske, A. P., "The four elementary forms of sociability: Framework for a unified theory of social relations," *Psychological Review*, 99, 4, 1992, pp. 689-723.
91 Chesney, D., L., and Seyfarth, R., M., "The representation of social relations by monkeys," *Cognition*, 37, 1990, pp. 167-196.
92 Pinker, S., *How the Mind Works*. New York: W. W. Norton & Company, 1997.
93 Allison, T., Puce, A., and McCarthy, G., "Social perception from visual cues: Role of the STS region," *Trends in Cognitive Science*, 4, 2000, pp. 267-278.
94 Birbaum, M., H., and Jou, J., W., "A theory of comparative response times and "difference" judgments," *Cognitive Psychology*, 22, 1990, pp. 184-210.
95 Moyer, R. S., Bradley, D. R., Sorensen, M. H., Whiting, C., and Mansfield, D. P., "Psychophysical functions for perceived and remembered size," *Science*, 200, 1978, pp. 330-332.
96 Koechlin, E., Naccahe, L., Block, E., and Dehaene, "Primed numbers: Exploring the modularity of numerical representations with masked and unmasked semantic priming," *Journal of Experimental Psychology: Human Perception and Performance*, 25, 6, 1999, pp. 1882-1905.
97 Chiao, Joan Y., Bordeaux, Andrew O., and Ambady, Nalimi, "Mental representations of social status," *Cognition*, 93, 2004, pp. B49-B57.
98 Ibid, B.56.
99 Chiao, Joan Y., Harada, Tokiko, Oly, Emily R., Li, Zhang, Parrish, Todd, and Bridge, Donna, "Neural representations of social status hierarchy in human inferior parietal cortex," *Neuropsychological*

100 Weber, max, *Economy and Society*, Berkeley, Los Angeles, CA: University of California, 1968.

101 Chan, Tak Wing, and Gold Thorpe, John H., "Is there a status order in contemporary British society?", *European Sociological Review*, 20, 5, 2004, pp. 383-401.

102 Chan, Tak Wing and Goldthorpe, john H., "Class and Status: The conceptual distinction and its empirical relevance," *American Sociological Review*, 72, 2007, p. 515.

103 Turner, Bryan S., *Status*, Minneapolis: University of Minnesota Press, 1988, p.67.

104 Anderson, C., John, O.P., Keltner, D., and Kring, A.M., "Who attains social status? Effects of personality and physical attractiveness in social groups," *Journal of Personality and Social Psychology*, 1, 81, 2001, pp. 116-132

105 Bales, R. F., "Channels of communication in small groups," *American Sociological Review*, 16, 1951, pp. 461-468.

106 Schein, E., *Organizational Culture and Leadership*. San Francisco: Jossey-Bass, 1985.

107 Anderson, B., Berger, J., Cohen, B.P., and Zelditch Jr., M., "Status classes in organizations", *Administrative Science Quarterly*, 2, 11, 1966, pp. 264-283.

108 Hallett, T., "Symbolic power and organizational culture," *Sociological Theory*, 21, 2003, pp. 128-149.

109 Magnas, M., "What's in a title? Plenty," *Personnel Journal*, 67, 1988, pp. 23-27.

110 Benoit-Smullyan, "Status, status types and status interrelations," *American Sociological Review*, 9, 1944, p. 160.

111 Back, K., Festinger, L., Hymovitch, B., Kelly, H., Schachter, S., and Thibault, J., "The methodology of studying rumor transmission," *Human Relations*, 3, 1950, pp. 307-312.

112 Goldberg, L., R., "The structure of phenotypic personality traits," *American Psychologist*, 48, 1993, pp. 26-34.

113 Mazur, A., "A biological model of status in face-to-face primate groups," *Social Forces*, 64, 1985, pp. 377-402.

114 Caspi, A., and Bern, D., J., "personality continuity and change across the life course." In Pervin, L. A. (Ed.), *Handbook of Personality: theory and Research*, NY: Guilford Press, 1990, pp. 549-575.

115 Berger, J., Cohen, B. P., and Zelditch, M., "Status characteristics and social interaction," *American Sociological Review*, 37, 1972, pp. 241-255.

116 Caspi, A., and Bern, D. J., Personality continuity and change across the life course", op.cit.

117 Judge, T., Higgins, C., Thorsen, C., and Barrick, M., "The big five personality traits, general mental ability, and career success across the life span," *Personal Psychology*, 52, 1999, pp. 621-652.

118 Helson, R., and Roberts, B., "The personality of young adult couples and wifes' work patterns," *Journal of Personality*, 60, 1992, pp. 575-597.

119 Anderson, Cameron, John, Oliver, P., Dacher, Keltner, and Kring, Ann M., "Who attains social status? Effects of personality and physical attractiveness in social groups," *Journal of Personality and Social Psychology*, 81, 1, 2001, pp. 116-132.

120 Arvey, R., Rotundo, M., Johnson, W., Zhang, Z., and McGee, M., "The determinants of leadership role occupancy: genetic and personality factors," *The Leadership Quarterly*, 17, 2006, pp. 1-20.

121 Hogan, R., Curphy, G. J., and Hogan, J., "What we know about leadership: Effectiveness and personality," *American Psychologist*, 49, 1994, pp. 493-504.

122 Judge, T., Bono, J., Ilies, R., and Gerhardt, M., "Personality and leadership: A qualitative and quantitative review," *Journal of Applied Psychology*, 87, 2002, pp. 621-657.

123 Harms, P., D., Roberts, Brent W., and Wood, Dustin, "Who shall lead? An integrative personality approach to the

study of the antecedents of status in informal social organizations," *Journal of Research in Personality*, 41, 2007, pp. 689-699.

124 Segal, D., R., Segal, M., W., and Koke, D., "Status inconsistency and self-evaluation," *Sociometry*, 33, 1970, pp. 347-57.

125 Singh-Manoux, A., Adler, N. E., and Marmot, M., G., "Subjective social status: its determinants and its association with measures of ill-health in the Whitehall II study," *Social Science Med*, 56, 2003, pp. 1321-33.

126 Sing-Manoux, A., Marmot, M. G., and Adler, N., E., "Does subjective social status predict health and change in health status better than objective status?" *Psychomatic Medicine*, 67, 2005, pp. 855-6.

127 Gianaros, P. J., Horenstein, J. A., Cohen, S., "Perigenual anterior cingulated morphology covaries with perceived social standing," *Social Cognitive and Affective Neuroscience*, 2, 2007, pp. 161-73.

128 Pezawas, L., Meyer-Linderberg, A., Drabant, E. M., "5-HTTLPR polymorphism impacts human cingulated-amygdala interaction: Genetic susceptibility mechanism for depression," *Nature Neuroscience*, 8, 2005, pp. 828-34.

129 Edwards, D., H., and Kravitz, A., "Serotonin, social status, and aggression," *Current Opinion in Neurobiology*, 7, 1997, pp. 812-9.

130 Rege, Mari, "Why do people care about social status?" *Journal of Economic behavior and Organizations*, 66, 2008, pp. 233-242

131 Frank, R., "The demand for non-observable and other non-positional goods," *American Economic Review*, 75, 1985, pp. 101-116.

132 Fang, H., "Social culture and economic performance," *American Economic Review*, 91, 2001, pp. 924-937.

133 Resendorfer, W., "Design innovation and fashion cycles," *American Economic Review*, 85, 1995, pp. 771-792.

134 Cole, H.L., Mailath, G.T., and Postlewaite, A., "Social norms, savings behavior, and growth," *Journal of Political Economy* , 100, 1992, pp. 1092-1125.
135 Cole, H. L., Mailath, G. J., and Postlewaite, A., "Incorporating concern for relative wealth with economic models," *Federal reserve Bank of Minneapolis Quarterly Review*, 19, 1995, pp.12-21.
136 Corneo, G., and Jeanne, O., "Social organization, status and saving Behaviour," *Journal of Public Economics*, 70, 1, 1996, pp. 37-52
137 Frank, Robert H., *Choosing the Right Pond Oxford: Oxford University press, 1985, p.137.*
138 Ireland, Norman J., "On limiting the market for status signals," *Journal of Public Economics*, 53, 1994, pp. 91-110.
139 Weber. Max. M., *The Protestant Ethic and the Spirit of Capitalism*, NY: Charles Scribner's Sons, 1958, p.53
140 Keynes, John M., *The Economics Consequences of the Peace*, London: St Martin's Press, 1971, pp. 11-12.
141 Bakshi, Gurdip S., and Chen, Zhiou, "The spirit of capitalism and stock-market prices," *The American Economic Review*, March 1996, pp. 133-157.
142 Hopkins, Ed, and Kornienko, Tatiana, "Running to keep in the same place: Consumer choice as a game of status," *The American Economic Review*, 4, 94, 2004, pp. 1085-1107.
143 Ibid, p. 1086.
144 Barnett, Wiiliam P., and Hansen, Porten T., "The red Queen in organizational evolution," *Strategic Management Journal*, 17, 1996, pp. 139-157.
145 Park, Robert Erza, and Burgess, Ernest Watson, *Introduction to the Science of Sociology*, Chicago, IL: University of Chicago Press, 1921, p.711.
146 Phillips, Damon J., and Zuckerman, Erza W., "Middle-status conformity: Theoretical restatement and empirical demonstration in two markets" *Research Paper No*

1598R, graduate School of Business, Stanford University, February 2001.

147 Hollamder, E. P., "Conformity, Status, and Idiosyncrasy credit," *Psychological Review*, 65, 1958, pp. 117-127.

148 Hollabder, E. P., "Competence and conformity in the acceptance of influence," *Journal of Abnormal and Social Psychology*, 61, 1960, pp. 365-369.

149 Dittes, James E., and Kelly, Harold H., "Effects of different conditions of acceptance upon conformity to group norms," *Journal of Abnormal and Social Psychology*, 53, 1956, pp. 100-107.

150 Philips, Damon J., and Zuckerman, Ezra W., "Middle-status conformity: Theoretical restatement and empirical demonstration in two markets," *American Journal of Sociology*, 107, 2001, pp. 379-429.

151 Homans, George C., *Social Behavior: Its Elementary Forms*. New York: Harcourt, brace and World. 1961, pp. 357-358.

152 Becker, Marshall H., "Sociometric location and innovativeness: Reformulation and extension of the diffusion model," *American Sociological Review*, 35, 1970, pp. 267-282.

153 Tittle, Charles R., Villemez, Wayne J., and Smith, Douglas A., "The myth of social class and criminality: An empirical assessment of the empirical evidence," *American Sociological Review*, 43, 1978, pp. 643-656.

155 Merton, R. K., "The Matthew effect in science, II: Cumulative advantage and the symbolism of intellectual property," *Isis*, 4, 79, 1988, p. 615.

156 Stuart, T., E., Ha, H., and Hybels, R. C., "Interorganizational endorsements and the performance of entrepreneurial ventures," *Administrative Science Quarterly*, 2, 44, 1999, pp. 315-349.

157 Phillips, D., J., "The promotion paradox: Organizational mortality and employee promotion chances in Silicon Valley law firms, 1946-1996," *American Journal of Sociology*, 4, 106, 2001, p. 1058.

158 Podolny, J. M., *Status Signals: A Sociological Study of Market Competition*, Princeton University press, Princeton, N.J., 2005.

159 Stuart, T. E., and Ding, W. W., "When do scientists become entrepreneurs? The social structural antecedents of commercial activity in the academic life sciences," *American Journal of Sociology*, 1, 112, 2006, pp. 97-144.

160 Ding, W. F., Murray, F., and Stuart, T. E., "Commercial science: A new arena for stratification in scientific careers" *Working Paper*, 2005.

161 Ding, W., Murray, F., and Stuart, T. E., "Gender differences in patenting in the academic life sciences," *Science*, 2006.

162 Bothner, Matthew S., Kim, Young-Kyu, and Smith, Edward Bishop," How does status affect performance? Status as an asset versus status as a liability in the PGA and NASCAR, *Working Paper*, University of Chicago.

163 Lovaglia, M. J., Lucas, J. W., Houser, L. A., Thye, S. R., and Markovsky, B., "Status processes and mental ability test scores," *American Journal of Sociology*, 1, 104, 1998, pp. 195-228.

164 Becker, H. S., *Outsiders: Studies in the Sociology of Deviance*, Free Press of Glencoe, London. 1963.

165 Merton, R. K., "The Matthew effect in science," *Science*, 38, 159, 1968, pp. 56-63.

166 Whyte, W. F., *Street Corner Society: The Social Structure of an Italian Slum*. Chicago: University of Chicago press, 1981.

167 Greenberg, Jerald, and Ornstein, Suzuyu, "High status job title as compensation for underpayment: a test of the equity theory," *Journal of Applied Psychology*, 2, 68, 1983, pp. 285-297.

168 Shils, E., *Center or Periphery: Essays in Macrosociology*, Chicago: University of Chicago Press, 1975.

169 DiMaggio, P., and Mohr, J., "Cultural capital, educational attainment, and mental selection," *American Journal of Sociology*, 90, 6, pp. 1231-61.

170 Goffman, E., "Symbols of class status," *British Journal of Sociology*, 2, 4, 1951, pp. 294-304.
171 Chan, Tak Wing, and Goldthorpe, John H., "Social status and newspaper readership," *American Journal of Sociology*, 111, 4, 2007, pp. 1095-1134.
172 Ibid, p.1130.
173 Ganzeboon, H. B., "Explaining differential participation in high-cultural activities: A confrontation of information processing and status-seeking theories," in *Theoretical Models and Empirical Analyses: Contributions to the explanation of Individuals Actions and Collective Phenomena*, edited by Raub, W. Utrecht: E. S. Publications, 1982.
174 Beck, U., *Risk Society: toward a New Modernity*. London: Sage, 1992.
175 Erickson, B. H., "Culture, class, and connections," *American Journal of Sociology*, 102, 1, 1996, pp. 217-51.
176 DiMaggio, P., "Classification in art," *American Sociological Review*, 52, 1987, p.445.
177 Stevens, A., and Price, J., *Evolutionary Psychiatry*. London: Routledge, 1996.
178 Nicholson, N., "How hardwired is human behavior?" *Harvard Business Review*, 76, 1998, pp. 135-147.
179 Conway, M., Difazio, R., and Mayman, S., "Judging other emotions as a function of others' status," *Social Psychology Quarterly*, 62, 1999, pp. 291-305.
180 Tiedens, L. Z., Ellsworth, P. C., and Mesquita, B., "Stereotypes of sentiments and status: Emotional expectations for high and low status group members," *Personality and Social Psychology Bulletin*, 26, 5, 200, pp. 560-575.
181 Keating, C. F., "Human dominance signals: the primate in us," In Ellyson, S. L., and Dovidio, J., F., (Eds.), *Power, Dominance and Nonverbal Behavior*. New York: Springer-Verlag, 1985, pp. 89-108.
182 Tiedens, Larissa Z., "Anger and advancement versus sadness and subjugation: The effect of negative emotion expressions in social status conferral," *Research*

Paper No 1615; graduate School of Business, Stanford University.

183 Barkow, J. H., *Darwin, Sex, and Status*, Toronto: University of Toronto Press, 1989, p.188.

184 Griskevivius, Vladas, Perea, Elaine F., Tybur, Joshua M., Gangestad, Stephen W., Shapiro, Jenessa R., and Kenrick, Douglas T., "Aggress to impress: hostility as an evolved context-dependent strategy," *Journal of Personality and Social Psychology*, 96, 5, 2009, pp. 980-994.

185 Treiman, D., *Occupational prestige in Comparative Perspective*, NY: Academic press, 1977.

186 Wiseman, R., M., and Gomez-Mejia, L. R., " A behavioral agency model of managerial risk taking," *Academy of Management Review*, 231, 1998, pp. 133-153.

187 Loch, Christoph, Yaziji, Michael, and Langen, Christian, "The fight for the alpha position: Channeling status competition in organizations," *European Management Journal*, 19, 2001, p.17.

188 Huberman, B. A., Lock, C. H., and Ongular, A., "Status as a Valued resource", *Working Paper*, 99/83/TM, INSEAD, 1999

189 Cialdini, R. B., *Influence-Science and Practice*, 3rd Edition, London: Harper Collins, London, 1993.

190 McGuire, M. T., and Raleigh, M. J., "Serotonin-behavior interactions in vervet monkeys," *Psychopharmacology Bulletin*, 21, 1985, pp. 458-467.

191 Booth, A., Shelley, G., Mazur, A., Thorp, G., and Kittok, M., "Testosterone, and winning and losing in human competition," *Hormones and Behavior*, December, 1989, pp. 556-571.

192 Frank, R. H., *Choosing the Right Pond*, Oxford: oxford University Press, 1985.

193 Ellingsen, Tore, and Johannesson, Magnus, "Paying respect," *Journal of Economic Perspectives*, 21, 4, 2007, pp. 135-149.

194 Markham, Steven E., Scott, K. Dow, and McKee, Gail H., "Recognizing good attendance: A longitudinal, quasi-experimental field study," *Personnel Psychology*, 55, 3, 2002, pp. 639-660.
195 Falk, Armin, and Ichino, Andrea, "Clean evidence on peer pressure," *Journal of Labor Economics*, 24, 1, 2006, pp. 39-57.
196 Stogdill, Ralph M., and Coons, Alvin E., (Eds.), *Leader Behavior: Its description and Measurement*, Columbus, OH: Bureau of Business Research, Ohio State University, 1957.
197 Carroll, Christopher D., "Why do the rich save so much?" in Stemrod, Joel (Ed.), *Does Atlas Shrug? The Economic Consequences of Taxing the Rich* (Harvard University Press: Cambridge, MA, 2000.
198 Carroll, Bertaut, and Starr-McClue, Martha, "Household portfolios in the United States," In *Household Portfolios*, (Ed.), Guiso, Luigi, Haliassos, Michael, and Japelli, Tullio. MIT Press, 2001.
199 Caroll, Christopher D., "Portfolios of the rich", op.cit.
200 Ibid.
201 Heaton, John C., and Lucas, Deborah J., "Portfolio choices and asset prices: The importance of entrepreneurial risk," *Journal of Finance*, 55, pp. 1163-1198.
202 Hall, Robert E., and Woodward, Susan E., *The Incentives to Start New Companies: Evidence from Venture Capital*, NBER: *Working paper 13056*, 2007.
203 Smith, Adam, *The Theory of Moral Sentiments*, Arlington House, 1969.
204 Veber, Max, *The Protestant Ethic and the Spirit of Capitalism*, New York: Charles Scribner and Sons, 1958.
205 Friedman, Milton, and savage, L. J., "The utility analysis of choices involving risk," *Journal of Political Economy*, 56, 1948, pp. 279-304.
206 Roussanov, Nikolai, "Diversification and its discontents: idiosyncratic and entrepreneurial risk in the quest for

social status," *Working Paper*, The Wharton School, university of Pennsylvania, 2009.

207 Becker, Gary S., Murphy, Kevin M., and Werning, Ivan," The equilibrium distribution of income and the market for status," *Journal of political Economy*, 113, pp. 282-310.

208 Cole, Harold, Mailath, George, and Postlewaite, Andrew, "Social norms, savings behavior and growth," *Journal of Political Economy*, 100, 1992, pp. 1092-1126.

209 Gullapalli, Diya, "Funds firms look to offer a toxic waste," *The Wall Street Journal*, Friday, march 27, 2009, p. C1.

210 Ridley, M., *The Red Queen*, NY: MacMillan, 1993.

211 Ellis, L., "Dominance and reproductive success among nonhuman animals: A cross-species comparison," *Ethology and Sociology*, 16, 1995, pp. 257-33

212 Low, B. S., Simon, C. P., and Anderson, K. G., "An evolutionary ecological perspective on demographic transitions: Modeling multiple currencies." *American Journal of Human Biology*, 14, 2002, pp. 149-167.

213 Dickermann, M., "Human reproductive plasticity," *Behavioral and Brain Sciences*, 16, 1993, p. 290.

214 Mueller, U., "The reproductive success of wealthy Americans," *Ethology and Sociology*, 5, 1984, pp. 45-49.
This evolutionary biology as an explanation of the behavior of contemporary humans is contested by those claiming that human reproductive behavior is a product of social learning alone.

215 Shiebekk, Vegard, "Fertility trends by social status, "Demographic *Research*, 18, 5, 2008, pp. 145-180.

216 Essock-Vitale, S. M., "The reproductive success of wealthy Americans," *Ethology and Sociology*, 5, 1984, pp. 45-49.

217 Mueller, U., and Mazur, "Evidence of unconstrained directional selection for male tallness," *Behavioral Ecology and Sociobiology*, 50, 2001, pp. 302-311.

218 Perusse, D., "Cultural and reproductive success in industrial societies: testing the relationship at the proximate

and ultimate levels," *Behavioral and Brain Sciences, 16, 1993, pp. 267-322.*

219 Kanazawa, S., "Can evolutionary psychology explain reproductive behavior in the contemporary United States?" *Sociological Quarterly*, 44, 203, pp. 291-301.

220 Ellis, L., "The biosocial female choice theory of social stratification," *Social Biology*, 48, 2001, pp. 298-320.

221 Trivers, R., and Williard, D., "Natural selection of parental ability to vary the sex ratio of offsprings," *Science*, 179, 1973, pp. 90-92.

222 Hewlett, Sylvia Ann, *Creating Life: What Every Woman Needs to Know about Having a baby and a career*, New York: Hyperion, 2003.

223 Dowd, Maureen, *Are Men Necessary*, New York: G. P. Putman's Sons, 2005.

224 Brown, Stephanie, and Lewis, Brian P., "Relational dominance and mate-selection criteria: Evidence that males attend to female dominance," *Evolution and Human Behavior*, 6, 25, 2004, pp. 406-415.

225 These views on SWANS are facing some criticisms. A 2005 article in the *American Journal of Sociology* finds that high=status and powerful women are rated as more attractive and are viewed as sexier than more subordinate women. In her book, *Why Smart Men Marry Smart Women* , Dr Christine B. Wheelan makes a case to prove that intelligent women can find a husband and happiness. That's a relief given that in James Brooks's "*SPANGLISH*", Adam Sandler, as a Los Angeles chef, falls for his hot Mexican maid, who is presented as the ideal woman.

226 Hopcroft, Rosemary L., "Sex status and reproductive success in the contemporary United States," *Evolution and Human Behavior*, 27, 2006, pp. 104-120.

227 Tocqueville, Alexix de, *Democracy in America*, Harper and Row, 1835, 1969, p. 274.

228 Harrington, Brooke, and Fine, Gary Alan, "opening the 'Black Box': Small groups and Twenty-First-Century

sociology, "Social *Psychology Quarterly*, 63, 4, 2000, pp. 312-23.

229 James, Rita M., "Status and Competence of Jurors," *American Journal of Sociology*, 64, 1959, pp. 563-70.

230 Strodtbeck, Fred L., James, Rita M., and Hawkins, Charles, "Social status and jury deliberations", *American Sociological Review*, 22, 1957, pp.713-19.

231 Op.cit.

232 Stodtbeck, Fred L., and Mann, Richard D., "Sex-role differentiation in jury deliberation," *Sociometry*, 19, 1956, pp. 3-11.

233 Hastie, Reid, Penrod, Steven D., and Pennington, Nancy, *Inside the Jury*, Harvard University press, 1983.`

234 Op.cit.

235 Ridgeway, Cecilia L., and Smith-Lovin, Lynn, "The gender system and interaction," *Annual Review of Sociology*, 25, 1999, pp. 191-216.

236 Brady, Henry E., Verba, Sidney, and Schlozman, Kay Lehman, "Beyond SES: A resource model of political participation," *The American Political Science Review*, 2, 89, 1995, pp. 271-94

237 York, Erin, and Cornwell, Benjamin, "Status on trial: Social characteristics and influence in the jury room," *Social Forces*, 1, 85, 2006, pp. 455-477.

238 Ibid, p. 470.

239 Landry, D., and Aronson, E., "The influence of the character of the criminal and his victim on the decisions of simulated jurors," *Journal of Experimental Social Psychology*, 5, 1969, pp. 141-152.

240 Dowdle, M., Gillen, H., and Miller, A., "Integration and attribution theories as predictors of sentencing by a simulated jury," *Personality and Social Psychology Bulletin*, 1, 1, 1974, pp. 270-272.

241 Sigall, H., and Ostrove, W., "Beautiful nut dangerous: Effects of offender attractiveness and nature of the crime on juridic judgment," *Journal of Personality and Social Psychology*, 31, 1975, pp. 410-414.

242 Veblen, T., *The Theory of the Leisure Class*, New York: Modern Library, 1899.

243 Duesenberry, J., *Income, saving, and the Theory of Consumer Behavior*, Cambridge University press, 1945.

244 Fisher, Walter H., "Durable consumption as status good: A study of neoclassical cases," *Institute for Advanced Studies*, November 2003.

245 Ibid.

246 Frank, R. H., "The demand for unobservable and other nonpositional goods," *American Economic review*, 1, 75, 1985, pp. 101-116.

247 Frank, R. H., "Frames of reference and the quality of life," *American Economic Review*, 2, 79, 1989, pp. 80-85.

248 Woersdorfer, Julia Sophie, "From status-seeking consumption to social norms: An application to the consumption of cleanliness," *Paper on Economics and Evolution*, (Ed.) *The Evolutionary Economics Group*, 2006, Jena, Germany.

249 Lavie, Moshik, "Show me the money: Status, cultural capital, and conspicuous consumption," *Universite de Paris I, 2008*.

250 Cole, H. L., Mailath, G. J., and Postlewaite, A., "Social norms, savings behavior, and growth," *Journal of Political Economy*, 100, 1992, pp. 1092-1125.

251 Cole, H. L., Mailath, G. J., and Postlewaite, A., "Incorporating concern for relative wealth into economic models," *Federal Reserve Bank of Minneapolis Quarterly Review*, 19, 1995, pp. 12-21.

252 Fremling, Gertrud, and Posner, Richard A., "Status, signaling and the law, with particular application to sexual harassment," *Working Paper, the Law School, University of Chicago*, p. 12.

253 Frank. R., "The demand for non-observable and other non-positional goods," *The American Economic Review*, 75, 1985, pp. 101-116.

254 Ibid.

255 Fang, H., "Social culture and economic performance," *American Economic Review*, 91, 2001, pp. 924-937.
256 Pesendorfer, W., "Design innovation and fashion cycles," *American Economic Review*, 85, 1995, pp. 771-792.
257 Cole, H. L., Mailath, G. J., Postlewaite, A., "Social status, savings behavior, and growth," *Journal of Political Economy*, 100, 1992, pp. 1092-1125.
258 Rege, mari., "Why do people care about social status?" *Journal of Economic behavior and Organization*, 66, 2008, pp. 233-242.
259 Ibid.
260 Alter, Adam L., and Forgas, Joseph P., "On being happy but fearing failure: The effects of mood on self-handicapping strategies," *Journal of Experimental Social Psychology*, 43, 2007, pp. 947-954.
261 Arkin, Robert M., and Baumgarden, A. H., "Self-handicapping," In *Attribution: Basic Issues and Applications*, (Eds), Harvey, J. H., and weary, G. W., Orlando, Fl: Academic Press, 1985, pp. 169-202.
262 Kolditz, Thomas A., and Arkin, Robert M., "An impression management interpretation of the self-handicapping strategy," *Journal of personality and Social Psychology*, 3, 43, 1982, pp. 492-502.
263 Berglas, Steven, and Jones, Edward E., "Drug choices as self-handicapping strategy in response to success," *Journal of Personality and Social Psychology*, 36, 1978, pp. 405-417.
264 Ibid.
265 Non-contingent results correspond to a situation where people receive successful feedback after attempting to solve insoluble problems and are, therefore, suspicious of the successful feedback.
266 Lucas, Jeffrey W., and Lovaglia, Michael, J. "Self-handicapping: gender, race, and status," *Current Research in Social Psychology*, 10, 10, 2005, pp. 235-249.
267 Ibid, p.243.

268 Frank, Robert H., "The demand for unobservable and other nonpositional goods," *American Economic Review*, 75, 1985, pp. 101-116.

269 Ireland, Norman J., "On limiting the market for status signals," *Journal of Public Economics*, 53, 1994, pp. 91-110.

270 Bagwell, Laurie S., and Bernheim, Douglas B., "Conspicuous consumption, pure profits, and the luxury tax," Mimeo, Princeton University, 1992.

271 Seidman, L., "Relativity and efficient taxation," *Southern Economic Journal*, 54, 1987, pp. 462-474.

272 Seidman, L., "The welfare cost of a relativistic economy," *Journal of Post-Keynesian Economics*, 11, 1988, pp. 295-304.

273 Ireland, Norman J., "Status-seeking income taxation and efficiency," *Journal of Public Economics*, 70, 1998, pp. 99-133.

274 Ibid.

275 Mazali. Rogerio, and Rodriguez-neto, Jose A., "Optimal taxation of status goods," *Working Paper*, Tulane University and University of Wisconsin, February 11, 2006.

276 Polodny, J. M., "Networks as the pipes and prisms of the market," *American Journal of Sociology*, 1, 107, 2001, pp. 33-60.

277 Grompers, P., and Lerner, J., *The Venture Capital Cycle*, Cambridge, MA: MIT Press, 2000.

278 Lerner, J., "The syndication of venture capital investments," *Financial Management*, 23, 3, 1994, pp. 16-27.

279 Stuart, T. E., Hoang, H., and Hybels, R. C., "Interorganizational endorsements and the performance of entrepreneurial ventures," *Administrative Science Quarterly*, 44, 1999, pp. 315-349.

280 Podolny, J. M., "A status-based model of market competition," *American Journal of Sociology*, 98, 1993, pp. 829-872.

281 Galaskiewicz, J., Bielefeld, W., and Dowell, M., "networks and organizational growth: A study of commu-

nity based nonprofits," *Administrative Science Quarterly*, 51, 2006, pp. 337-380.

282 Piskorski, J. M., "Network of power and status: reciprocity in the venture capital syndication market," *Working Paper*, Harvard Business School, Boston, MA, 2004.

283 Hochberg, Y., Ljungqvist, A. P., and Lu, Y., "Whom you know matters: venture capital networks and investment performance," *Journal of Finance*, 62, 20067. pp. 251-301.

284 Hsu, D. H., "What do entrepreneurs pay for venture capital affiliation?" *Journal of Finance*, 59, 2004, pp. 1805-1844.

285 Guler, Isin, and Guillen, Mauro F., "Home-country networks and foreign expansion," *Working Paper*, kenan-Flagler business School, University of Northern Carolina, 2008.

286 Bourdieu, P., and Wacquant, L. J. D., *An Invitation to Reflexive Sociology*, Chicago: University of Chicago Press, 1992, p. 119.

287 Bothner, Matthew S., Kang, jeong-Han, and Lee, Wonjae, "Status volatility and organizational growth in the U.S venture-capital industry," *Working Paper*, University of Chicago, 2009.

288 Dannemaier, W. D., and Thumin, F. T., "Authority status as a factor in perceptual distortion of size," *Journal of Social Psychology*, 63, 1964, pp. 361-365.

289 Wilson, P. R., "Perceptual distortion of height a function of ascribed status," *Journal of Social Psychology*, 74, 1968, pp. 97-102.

290 Ellis, L., "The high and mighty among men and beast: How universal is the relationship between men height (or body size) and social status," In Ellis, L., (Ed.), *Social stratification and economic inequality: Reproductive and interpersonal aspects of dominance and status*, Vol 2, Westport: Praeger, pp. 93-111.

291 Etcoff, N., *Survival of the Prettiest: The Science of Beauty*, NY: Doubleday, 1999.

292 McGinnis, J., *Selling of the President*, NY: Penguin, 1988.

293 Case, Anne, and Paxson, Christina, "Stature and status: Height, ability, and labor market outcomes," *Journal of Political Economy*, 3, 116, 2008, pp. 499-532.

294 Spearman, C., "General intelligence, objectively determined and measured," *American Journal of Psychology*, 15, 1904, pp. 201-293.

295 Jensen, A. R., *bias in Mental Destiny*, NY: Free press, 1980, pp. 340-341.

296 Jencks, C. *Inequality: A reassessment of the Effect of Family and schooling in America*, NY: Basic, 1972, pp. 220-281.

297 Reynolds, C. R., Chastain, R. L., Kaufman, A. S., and McLean, J. E., "Demographic characteristics and IQ among adults: Analysis of the WAIS-R standardization sample as a function of the stratification variables," *Journal of Social Psychology*, 25, 1987, pp. 323-342.

298 Waller, J. H., "Achievement and social mobility: relationships among IQ score, education, and occupation in two generations," *Social Biology*, 18, 1971, pp. 252-259.

299 Mascie-Taylor, C. G. N., and Gibson, T. B., "Social mobility and IQ components," *Journal of Biosocial Science*, 10, 1978, pp. 263-276.

300 Buss, D. M., *The Evolution of Desire: Strategies of Human Mating*, New York: Basic Books, 1994.

301 Graziano, W. G., Jensen-Campbell, L. A., Todd, M., and Finch, J. F., "Interpersonal attraction from an evolutionary psychology perspective: Women's reactions to dominant and prosocial men," In Simpson, J. A., and Kendrick, D. T.)Eds.), *Evolutionary Social Psychology*, Mahwah: Lawrence Erlbaum, 1997, pp. 141-167.

302 Gutierres, S. E., Kenrick, D. T., and Partch, J. J., "Beauty, dominance, and the mating game: Contrast effects in self-assessment reflect gender differences in mate

selection," *Personality and Social Psychology Bulletin*, 25, 1999, pp. 1126-1134.

303 Kenrick, D. T., Neuberg, S. L., Zierk, K. L., and krones, J. M., "Evolution and social cognition: Contrast effects as a function of sex, dominance, and physical attractiveness," *Personality and Social Psychology Bulletin*, 20, 1994, pp. 210-217.

304 Davis, K., "Intermarriage in caste societies," *American Anthropologist*, 43, 1941, pp. 376-395.

305 Elder, Jr., G. H., "Appearance and education in marriage mobility," *American Sociological Review*, 34, 1969, pp. 519-533.

306 Taylor, P. A., and Glenn, N. D., "The utility of education and attractiveness for female status attainment through marriage," *American Sociological Review*, 41, 1976, pp. 484-498.

307 Udry, J. R., "The importance of being beautiful," *American Journal of Sociology*, 83, 1984, pp. 154-160.

308 Hamermesh, D. S., and Biddle, J. E. " Beauty and the labor market," *American Economic Review*, 84, 1994, pp. 1174-1194.

309 Massey, Douglas, *Categorical Inequality*, Russell Sage Foundation, 2007.

310 Fisher, C. S., and Hout, M., *Century of Difference: How America Changed in the Last One Hundred Years*. New York: Russell sage Foundation, 2006.

311 Gossett, Thomas, F., *Race: The History of an Idea in America*. Oxford University press, 1997.

312 Gates, Jr., Henry louis, "The passing of Anatole Broyard", in *Thirteen Ways of Looking at a Black Man*, Random House, 1997, pp. 180-214.

313 Telles, Edward E., "Racial ambiguity among the Brazilian population," *Ethnic and Racial Studies*, 25, 3, 2002, pp. 415-41.

314 Eberhardt, Jennifer L., "Imaging race," *American Psychologist*, 60, 2005, pp. 181-90.

315 Allen, B. P., "African Americans' and European Americans' mutual attributions: Adjective generation technique stereotyping," *Journal of Applied Social Psychology*, 26, 1996, pp. 884-912.

316 Ronquillo, Jaclyn, "The effects of skin tone on race-related Amygdala activity: An FMRI investigation," *Social Cognition Affect Neuroscience*, 2, 2007, pp. 39-44.

317 Eberhardt, Jennifer L., Goff, Phillip Atiba., Purdie, Valena J., and Davies, Paul G., "Seeing black: race, crime, and visual processing," *Journal of Personality and Social Psychology*, 87, 6, 2004, pp. 876-893.

318 Saperstein, Alya, and Penner, Andrew, "Does social status shape race: The effects of changes in social position on racial classification and identification," *Working Paper*, Stanford, 2008.

319 Ibid, p. 27.

320 Pfeffer,J., "Organizational demography," in Staw, B., and Cummings, L., (Eds.), *Research in Organizational Behavior*, Greenwich, Connecticut: JAI Press, 5, 1983, pp. 299-357.

321 Beggs, J., "The institutional environment: Implications for race, gender inequality in the U. S. labor market," *American Sociological Review*, 60, 4, 1995, pp. 612-633.

323 Kumar, K., and Beyerlein, M., "Construction and validation of an instrument for measuring ingratiatory behaviors in organizational settings," *Journal of Applied psychology*76, 1991, pp. 619-627.

324 Gordon, R. A., "Import of ingratiatory on judgments and evaluation: A meta-analytic investigation," *Journal of Personality and Social Psychology*, 71, 1996, pp. 54-60.

325 Westphal, James D., and Stern, Ithai, "The other pathway to the boardroom: Interpersonal influence behavior as a substitute for elite credentials and majority status in obtaining board appointments," *Administrative Science Quarterly*, 51, 2006, pp. 169-204.

326 Ibid, p.194.

327 Burnstein, Eugene, "Book review: *Ingratiation: A social Psychological Analysis* by Jones, Edward E.", *The American Journal of Psychology*, *79*, 1, pp. 159-161.

328 Ridgeway, C., "The emergence of status beliefs: From structural inequalities in legitimizing ideology." In Jost, J., and Major, B.,) Eds.), *The Psychology of legitimacy: Emerging perspectives on ideology, Justice, and Intergroup Relations* New York: Cambridge University Press, 2001, pp. 257-277.

329 Feldman, Barrett, L., and Swim, J. K., "Appraisals of prejudice and discrimination," In Swim, J. K., and Stangor, C., (Eds.), *Prejudice: The target's Perspective*. San Diego, CA: Academic press, 1998, pp. 11-36.

330 Sedikides, C., and Skowronski, J. J., "The law of cognitive structure activation," *Psychological Inquiry*, 2, 1991, pp. 169-184.

331 Inman, M. L., and baron, R. S., "Influence of prototypes on perception of prejudice," *Journal of Personality and Social Psychology*, *70*, 1996, pp. 727-739.

332 Crocker, J., and Major, B., "Social stigma and self-esteem: the self-protective properties of stigma," *Psychological Review*, *96*, 1989, pp. 608-630.

333 Crosby, F., Pufall, A., Snyder, R. C., O'Connell, M., and Whalen, P., "The denial of personal disadvantage among you, me, and all the other ostriches," In Crawford, M., and gentry, M., (Eds.), *Gender's Thought: Psychological Perspectives*. New York: Springer-Verlag, 1989, pp. 79-99.

334 Branscombe, N. R., "Thinking about one's gender group's principles or disadvantages: Consequences for well-being in women and men," *British Journal of Social Psychology*, *37*, 1998, pp. 167-184.

335 Major, Brenda, Gramzow, Richard H., McCoy, Shannon K., Levin, Shana, Schrader, Toni, and Sidanius, Jim, "Perceived personal discrimination: The role of group status and legitimizing ideology," *Journal of Personal and Social Psychology*, 82, 3, 2002, pp. 269-282.

336 Schmader, T., Major, B., Eccleston, C. P., and McCoy, S. K., "Devaluing domains in response to threatening intergroup comparisons: Perceived legitimacy and the status value asymmetry," *Journal of personality and Social Psychology*, 80, 2001, pp. 782-796.

337 Bylsma, W. H., Major, B., and Cozzarelli, C., "The influence of legitimacy appraisals on the determinants of entitlement beliefs," *Basic and Applied Social Psychology*, 17, 1995, pp. 223-237.

338 Jost, T. T., and Burgess, D., "Attitudinal ambivalence and the conflict between group and system justification motives in low status groups," *Personality and Social Psychology Bulletin*, 26, 2000, pp. 293-305.

339 Ellemers, N., Wilke, H., and Van Knippenberg, A., "Effects of the legitimacy of low group or individual status on individual and collective status-enhancement strategies," *Journal of Personality and Social Psychology*, 64, 1993, pp. 766-778.

340 Major, B., "From social inequality to personal entitlement: The role of social comparisons, legitimacy appraisals, and group membership," In Zanna, M. P., (Ed.), *Advances in Experimental Social psychology Bulletin*, 76, 1994. San Diego, CA: Academic press, pp. 293-348.

341 Moscovici, S., "Social consciousness and its history," *Culture and Psychology*, 4, 1998, pp. 411-429.

342 Klengel, J. A., and Smith, E. R., *Beliefs about Inequality: Americans' View of What Is and What Ought to Be*. Hawthorne, NJ: Aldine de Gruyer, 1986.

343 Crandall, C. S., "prejudice against fat people: ideology and self interest," *Journal of Personality and Social Psychology*, 66, 1994, pp. 882-894.

344 Sidanius, J., and Pratto, F., "Social dominance: An intergroup theory of social hierarchy and oppression," In Sniderman, P., and Tetlock, P. E., (Eds.), *Prejudice, Politics, and race in America Today*. Stanford, CA: Stanford University press, 1993, pp. 381-401.

345 Klengel, J. R., and Smith, E. R., *Beliefs about Inequality: Americans' View of What Is and What Ought to Be*, Ibid.
346 Tajfel, H., "Social psychology of intergroup relations," *Annual Review of Psychology*, 53, 1982, pp. 1-39.
347 Wright, S. C., Taylor, D. M., and Moghaddam, F. M., "Responding to membership in a disadvantaged group: From acceptance to collective protest," *Journal of Personality and Social Psychology*, 58, 1990, pp. 994-1003.
348 Schmader, T., major, B., Eccleston, C. P., and McCoy, "Devaluing domains in response to threatening intergroup comparisons: perceived legitimacy and the status value asymmetry," *Journal of Personality and Social Psychology*, 80, 2001, pp. 782-796.
349 Kimura, D., *Sex and Cognition*, MIT Press, Boston, MA, 200.
350 Gouchie, C. T., and Kimura, D., "The relationship between testosterone and cognitive ability patterns," *Psyhconeuroendocriniology*, 16, 1991, pp. 323-334.
351 Wingfield, J. C., Ball, G. F., Duffy, A. M., and Hegner, R. E., "Testosterone and aggression in birds," *American Science*, 75, 1987, pp. 602-608.
352 Mazur, A., and Booth, A., "Testosterone and dominance in men," *Behavioral Brain Science*, 21, 1998, pp. 353-397.
353 Ibid.
354 Schultheiss, O. C., Dargel, A., and Rohde, W., "Implicit power motivation moderates men's testosterone responses to imagined and real dominance success," *Hormones and Behavior*, 36, 1999, pp. 234-241.
355 Josephs, R. A., Newman, M.L., Brown, R. P., and Beer, J. M., "Status, testosterone, and human intellectual performance: stereotype threat as a status concern," *Psychological Science*, 14, 2003, pp. 158-163.
356 Newman, Matthew L., Guin Sellers, Jennifer, and Josephs, Robert A., "Testosterone, cognition, and social status," *Hormones and Behavior*, 47, 2005, pp. 205-211.

357 Josephs, Robert A., and Guinn Sellers, Jennifer, "The mismatch effect: when testosterone and status are at odds," *Journal of Personality and Social Psychology*, 90, 6, 2006, pp. 999-1013.

358 Merton, Robert K., "The Matthew Effect in science," *Science*, 159, 1968, pp. 56-63.

359 Gould, Roger V., "The origins of status hierarchies: A formal theory and empirical test," *American Journal of Sociology*, 107, 2002, p. 1143.

360 Podolny, Joel M., *Status Signals: A Sociological Study of Market Competition*. Princeton, NJ: Princeton University Press, 2005.

361 Zuckerman, Ezra W., and Kim, Tai-Young, "The critical trade-off: identity assignment and box-office success in the feature film industry," *Industrial and Corporate Change*, 12, 2003, pp. 27-67.

362 Bothner, Matthew, and Haynes, Richard, "When do Matthew Effects occur?" *Journal of Mathematical Sociology*, Forthcoming.

363 Coser, Lewis A., "The political functions of eunuchism," *American Sociological Review*, 2, 29, 1964, pp. 880-885.

364 Merton, Robert K., "The Matthew Effect in science," op. cit.

365 Bothner, Matthew S., Podolny, Joel M., and Smith, Edward Bishop, "Organizing contests for status: The Matthew Effect versus the Mark Effect," *Management Science, 2009.*

367 Ibid.

368 Frank, R. H., *Choosing the Right Pond*, Ibid.

369 Geertz, C., *Peddlers and Princes: Social development and Economic Change in two Indonesian Towns*. Chicago: the University of Chicago press. 1963.

370 Portes, A., "Social capital: Its origins and applications in modern sociology," *Annual Review of Sociology*, 24, 1998, pp. 1-24.

371 Buss, D. M., "Sex differences in human mate preferences: Evolutionary hypotheses tested in 37 cultures," *behavior and Brain Science*, 12, 1989, pp. 1-49.

372 Twosend, J. M., "mate selection criteria: A pilot study," *Ethology and Sociobiology*, 10, 1989, pp. 241-253.

373 Buss, D. M., "mate preference mechanisms: Consequences for partner choice and intrasexual competition." In Barkow, J. H., Cosmides, L, and Tooby, J., (Eds.), *The Adapted mind: Evolutionary Psychology and the generation of Culture*, New York: oxford University Press, 1992, pp. 249-266.

374 For example, male-male homicide rates increase with inequality, suggesting that young men's minds are designed to upregulate motivations to take competitive risks when they feel that their mating opportunities are limited by lack of resources. See, Daly, M., Wilson, M., and Vasden, S., "Income inequality and homicide rates in Canada and the United States," *Canadian Journal of Criminology*, 43, 2001, pp. 219-236.

375 Ermen. Elsa, Cosmides. Leda, and Tooly, John, "Relative Status regulates risky decision making in men: Evidence for the co-evolution of motivation and cognition," *Evolution and Human Behavior*, 29, 2008, pp. 106-118.

376 Ibid, p.115.

377 Tiedens, L. Z., Ellsworth, P. C., and Mesquita, B., "Stereotypes about sentiments and status: Emotional expectations for high- and low-status group members," *Personality and Social psychology Bulletin*, 26, 5, 2000, pp. 560-574.

378 Sande, G. N., Ellard, J. H., and Ross, M., "Effect of arbitrarily assigned status labels on self-perceptions and social perceptions: the mere position effect," *Journal of Personality and Social Psychology.*, 50, 4, 1986, pp. 684-689.

379 Magee, Joe C., and Galinsky, Adam D., "Social hierarchy: the self-reinforcing nature of power and status," *The .Academy of Management Annals*, 2, 1, 2008, pp. 351-398.

380 Langer, E. J., and Abelson, R. P., "A patient by any other name...: Clinician group differences in labeling bias," *Journal of Consulting and Clinical Psychology, 42, 1974, pp. 4-9.*

381 Humphrey, R., "How work roles influence perception: Structural-cognitive processes and organizational behavior," *American Sociological Review*, 50, 2, 1985, pp. 242-252.

382 Sande, G. N., Ellard, J. H., and Ross, M., "Effects of arbitrarily assigned status labels on self-perceptions and social perceptions: The mere position effect," Ibid

383 Darley, J. M., and Gross, P. H., "A hypothesis-confirming bias in labeling effects," *Journal of Personality and Social psychology*, 44, 1, 1983, pp. 20-33.

384 New York Times, March 30, 2002, p. A13.

385 Kumru, C., and Vesterlund, L., "The effects of status on voluntary contributions," *University of South Wales Working Paper*, 2005.

386 Munoz-Garcia, Felix, "Competition for status acquisition in public good games," *University of Pittsburg Working Paper*, 2008.

387 Hopkins, E., and Kornienko, T., "Running to keep in the same place: Consumer choice as a game of status," *American Economic Review*, 9, 2004, pp. 1085-1107.

388 Wiener, M., *English Culture and the Decline of the Industrial Spirit 1850-1980*, Cambridge: Cambridge University Press, 1981.

389 Fershtman, C., and Weiss, Y., "Social status, culture and economic performance," *Economic Journal*, 103, 1993, pp. 946-59.

390 Fershtman, Chiam, Murphy, Kevin M., and Weiss, Yoram, "Social status, education, and growth," *Journal of Political Economy*, 104, 1996, pp. 108-132.

391 Hirsch, Fred, *Social limits to Growth*, Cambridge, Mass: Harvard University press, 1976.

392 Cole, Harold L., Mailath, George J., and Postlewaite, Andrew, "Social norms, savings behavior, and growth," *Journal of Political Economy*, 100, 1992, pp. 1092-1125.
393 Arrow, K., "political and economic evaluation of social effects and externalities," In *Frontier of Quantitative Economics*, Ed. Intriligator, M., Amsterdam: North Holland, 1971.
394 Veblen, Thorstein, *The Theory of the leisure Class: An Economic Study of Institutions*. London: Unwin Books, 1899; reprinted New York: Dover Publications, 1994.
395 Ibid, p. 24.
396 Ibid, p. 71.
397 White, Joseph B., "Yes, people buy Ferraris in a recession," *The Wall Street Journal*, March 31, 2009, p. D3.
398 Aeppel, Timothy, "BMW, despite success, is acting like it is under siege," *The Wall Street Journal*, 19, February 1992, p. B4.
399 The Economist, "The luxury-goods trade," 8 January 1993, p. 98.
400 Witt, Howard, "La. Sleaze Easily Tops Illinois," *The Chicago Tribune*, Friday, March 27, 2009, p.4.
401 Besley, T., and Mclaren, J., "Taxes and bribery: The role of wage incentives," *The Economic Journal*, Vol 13, 1993, No. 416, pp. 119-141.
402 Galiani, Sebastian, and Weinschelbaum, "Social status and corruption," *Working Paper*, Washington University of St Louis, April 21, 2007.
403 Ibid.
404 Konstantopoulous, Stasinos," What's in a Name?" IIT, NCSR 'Demokritis.
405 Ibid, p.6.
406 Epstein, Joseph, "Uncle Bernie and the Jews," *Newsweek*, January 10, 2009.
407 Anstis, S.M., Mayhow, J. W., and Morley, T., "The perception of where a face or television 'portrait' is looking," *American Journal of Psychology*, 82, 1969, pp. 474-489.

408 Langton, S. R. H., Watt, R. J., Bruce, V., "Do the Eyes have it? Cues to the direct of social attention," *Trends in Cognitive Science*, 4, 2, 2000, pp. 50-59.

409 Tomasello, M., Call, J., and hare, A., "Five primate species follow the gaze of con-specifics," *Animal Behavior*, 55, 1998, pp. 1063-1069.

410 Shepherd, Stephen V., Deaner, Robert O., and Platt, Michael L., "Social status gates social attention in monkeys," *Current Biology*, February 21, 2006, R119- R120.

411 Examples of *nostalgie de la boue* are the Lady Chatterly syndrome, where genteel women fall for a "bit of rough". When Constance confesses to her husband that she is pregnant with Mellors' child he rails at her about the "beastly lowness of women' and then goes to say: 'That proves that what I've always thought about you is correct: you are not normal, you're not in your right senses. You're one of those half-insane, perverted women who must run after depravity, the nostalgie de la boue.'

412 McElroy, J., Morrow, P., "Personal space, personal appearance, and personal selling," *Psychological Reports*, 74, 1994, pp. 425-26.

413 Guegen, N., and Pichot, N., "The influence of status on pedestrians' failure to observe a road-safety rule," *The Journal of Social Psychology*, 3, 141, pp. 413-415.

414 Harris, M., "Mediators between frustration and aggression in a field experiment," *Journal of Experimental Social Psychology*, 10, 1974, pp. 561-571,

415 Solnick, P., and Shaw, J., "Is defendant status a liability or a shield? Crime severity and professional relatedness," *Journal of Applied Psychology*, 24, 1994, pp. 1877-1836.

416 A similar result showed that people are more tolerant to high status criminals than to neutral status ones. See Gray, D., and Ashmore, R., "Biasing influence of defendants' characteristics on simulated sentencing," *Psychological Reports*, 38, 1976, pp. 727-738.

417 Guegen, Nicjolas, and Pascual, Alexander, "Status and people's tolerance towards ill-mannered person: A field study," *Journal of Mundane Behavior*, 4, 1, 2003, pp. 1-8.

418 Ibid, p.8.

419 Becker, E., *The Denial of Death*, New York: Free press, 1973

420 Reinsch, Jessica R., and Spotanski, Cory L., "Human territoriality: Affect of status on personalization and demarcation," *Journal of Psychological Inquiry*, 10, 2005, pp. 16-21.

421 Ibid.

422 Eagly, A. H., *Sex Differences in Social Behaviour: A Social-Role Interpretation*. Hillsdale, NJ: Erlbaum, 1987.

423 Mohiuddin, Yasmeen, "Country rankings by the status of women index," *Working Paper*, The 1966 Conference of the International Association for Feminist Economics, July 21-23, 1996.

424 Bettencourt, B. A., and Miller, N., "Gender differences in aggression as a function of provocation: A meta-analysis," *Psychology Bulletin*, 119, 1996, pp. 422-447.
Eagly, A. H., and Steffen, V. J., "Gender and aggressive behaviour" A meta-analytic review of the social psychological literature, *Psychological Bulletin*, 100, 1986, pp. 309-330.

425 Rhoodie, E. M., *Discrimination against Women: A Global Survey*. Jefferson, NJ: McFarland, 1989,

426 Conway, Michael, Irannyard, Shahrzad, and Giannopolous, Constantina, "Status-based expectancies for aggression, with regard to gender differences in aggression in social psychological research," *Aggressive Behavior*, 31, 2005, pp. 381-398.

427 Ibid, p. 396.

428 Argyle, M., *The Psychology of Social Class*. New York: Routledge, 1994.

429 Dittman, H., Mannetti, L., and Semin, G. R., "fine feathers make fine birds: A comparative study of the impact of

material wealth on perceived identities in England and Italy, "Social *Behaviour*, 4, 1989, pp. 195-200.

430 Conway, M., Pizzamiglio, M. T., and Mount, L., "Status, communality and agency: Implications for the stereotypes of gender and other groups," *Journal of Personality and Social Psychology*, 71, 1996, pp. 25-38.

431 Geis, F. L., Brown, V., Jennings, J., and Cornado-Taylor, D., "Sex vs. Status in sex-associated stereotypes," *Sex Roles*, 11, 1984, pp. 771-785.

432 Conway, Michael, and Vartanian, Lenny, R., "A status account of gender stereotypes: beyond communality and agency, "Sex *Roles*, 43, ¾, 2000, pp. 181-199.

433 Berger, J., Wagner, D. G., and Zelditch, M., "Introduction. Expectation states theory: review and assessment," In Berger, J, and Zelditch, M., *Status rewards, and Influence: How Expectations Organize Behavior*. San Francisco: Jossey-bass, 1985, pp. 1-72.

434 Dovidio, J. F., Ellyson, S. L., Keating, C. F., Heltman, K., and brown, C. E., "The relationship of social power to visual displays of dominance between men and women," *Journal of Personality and Social Psychology*, 54, 1985, pp. 233-242.

435 Wood, W., and Karten, S. J., "Sex differences in interaction style as a product of perceived sex differences in competence," *Journal of Personality and Social Psychology*, 50, 1986, pp. 341-347.

436 Geis, F. L., "Self-fulfilling prophecies: A social psychology view of gender," In Beall, A. E., and Sternberg, R. J., (Eds.), *The Psychology of Gender*, New York: Guilford press, 1993, pp. 9-54.

437 Conway, Michael, and Vartarian, Lenny R., "A status account of gender stereotypes beyond communality and agency," op. cit., p. 197.

438 *Merriam-Webster's Collegiate Dictionary*, Springfield, MA: Merriam-Webster, 10th Ed., 1993, p. 1315.

439 Conway, Michael, Wood, Wendy-Jo, Dugan, Michael, and Pushkar, Dolores, "Are women perceived as

engaging in more maladaptive worry than men? A status interpretation," *Sex Roles*, 49, ½, 2003, pp. 1-10.
440 Brody, L. R., and Hall, J. A., "Gender and emotion," in Lewis, M., and Havilland-Jones, J. M., (Eds), *Handbook of Emotions*, 2nd Ed., New York: Guilford, 2000, pp. 338-349.
441 Spence, J. T., Helmreich, R. L., and Holahan, C. K., "Negative and positive components of psychological masculinity and femininity and their relationship to self-reports of neurotic and acting behaviors," *Journal of personality and Social Psychology*, 37, 1979, pp. 1673-1682.
442 Eagly, A. H., Wood, W., and Diekman, A. B., "Social role theory of sex differences and similarities: A current appraisal," In Eckles, T., and Trautner, H. M., (Eds.), *The Development of Social Psychology of Gender* London: Erlbaum, 2000, pp. 123-174.
443 Conway, Michael, et al., Op Cit., p. 7.
444 Davidson, D. J., and Frendenburg, W. R., "Gender and environmental risk concerns- A review and analysis of available research," *Environment and Behavior*, 28, 3, 1996, pp. 302-339.
445 Flynn, J., Slovic, P., and Mertz, C. K., "Gender, race, and perceived risk," *Risk Analysis*, 14, 6, 1994, pp. 1101-1108.
446 Finucane, M. L., Slovic, P., Mertz, C. K., Flynn, J., and Satterfied, T. A., "Gender, race, and perceived risk: The 'White Male' effect", *Health, Risk and Society*, 2, 2, 2000, p. 159-172.
447 Palmer, C. G. S., "Risk perception: Another look at the 'white male' effect," *Health, Risk, and Society*, 5, 1, 2003, p. 71.
448 Kahan, Dan M., Braman, Donald, Gastil, John, Slovic, Paul, and Mertz, C. K., "Culture and identity-protective cognition: explaining the white male effect in risk perception," *Journal of Empirical Legal Studies*, 4, 3, 2007, pp. 465-505.

449 Evans-Pritchard, E. E., *The Neur: A Description of the Modes of Livelihood and Political Institutions of Nilotic People*. Oxford, 1940, p. 85.
450 Akerlof, G., "Labor contracts as a partial gift exchange," *Quarterly Journal of Economics*, 87, 4, 1982, pp. 543-569.
451 Mauss, M., *The Gift*. Routledge, London, 1925. (Reprinted in 1990), p. 42.
452 Palatteau, Jean-Philippe, and Sekeris, Petros G., "On the feasibility of power and status ranking in traditional setups," *Center for Research in the Economics of Development, Working Paper*, November 2001.
453 Hollander, H., "A social exchange approach to voluntary cooperation," *The American Economic Review*, 80, 5, 1990, pp. 1157-1167.
454 Van de Ven, J., "The demand for social approval and status as a motivation to give," *Journal of Institutional and Theoretical Economics*, 158, 3, 2002, pp. 464-482.
455 Blau, Peter M., *Exchange and Power in Social Life*. New Brunswick, NJ: Transaction Publishers, 1964.
456 Homans, George C., *Social behavior: Its Elementary Forms*. New York: Harcourt, Brace and Jovanovich, Inc, 1961, p. 258.
457 Lovaglia, Michael, and Houser, Jeffrey," Emotional reactions, status characteristics, and social interaction," *American Sociological Review*, 61, 1996, pp. 867-883.
458 Bianchi, Alison, Lancianese, Donna, and Hunter, Vicki, "Gifts and social status: On-going experimental tests of behavior-status and social exchange theories," *Kent State University Working Paper*, 2009.
459 Thorne, Barrie, Kramarae, Cheris, and Henley, Nancy, "Language, gender and society: Opening a second decade of research," In *Language, gender, and Society*, (Eds), Thorne, B., Kramarae, Cheris, and hneley,N. Rowley, MA: Newbury House, 1983, pp. 7-24.
460 Ridgeway, C., *The Dynamics of Small Groups*. NY: st. Martin's, 1983.

461 Ridgeway, C., and Berger, J., "Expectations, legitimizing, and dominance Behavior in task groups," *American Sociological Review*, 51, 1986, pp. 603-17.
462 Kollock, P., Blumstein, P., and Schwartz, P., "Sex and power in interaction," *American Sociological Review*, 50, 1985, pp. 34-47.
463 Smith-Lovin, Lynn, and Brody, Charles, "Interruptions in group discussions: The effects of gender and group composition," *American Sociological Review*, 54, 1989, pp. 424-435.
464 Wagner, David G., Ford, Rebecca S., and Ford, Thomas W., "Can gender inequalities be reduced?" *American Sociological Review*, 51, 1986, pp. 47-61.
465 Okomato, Dina G., and Smith-Lovein, Lynn, "Changing the subject: Gender, status, and the dynamics of topic change," *American Sociological Review*, 66, 12, 2001, pp. 852-873.
466 Moscatelli, Silvia, Albarello, Flavia, and Rubini, Monica, "Linguistic discrimination in minimal groups," *Journal of Language and Social Psychology*, 22, 2, 2008.
467 Nah, Ieda E., "Expectation states: Are formal words a status cue for competence?" *Current research in Social Psychology*, 13, 5, 2007.
468 Prendergast, C., and Topel, R. H., "Favoritism in organizations," *Journal of Political Economy*, 104, 5, 1996, pp. 958-978.
469 Allport, G. W., *The Nature of Prejudice*. Cambridge, MA: Addison Wesley, 1958 (originally published in 1954).
470 McGuire, W. J., "Attitudes and attitude change," In Lindzey, G., and Aronson, E. (Eds.), *The Handbook of Social Psychology*, 3rd Ed., Vol 2. New York: Random house. P. 265.
471 Jahoda, G., Thompson, S. S., and Bhatt, S., "Ethnic identity and preferences among Asian immigrant children in Glasgow," *European Journal of Social psychology*, 2, 1972, pp. 19-32.

472 Gramski, A., *Selections from the Prison Notebooks*. New York: International Publishers, 1971.

473 Jost, J. T., and Banaji, M. R., "The role of stereotyping in system justification and the production of false consciousness," *British Journal of Social psychology*, 33, 1994, pp. 1-27.

474 Ibid.

475 Skevington, S., "Intergroup relations and nursing," *European journal of Social Psychology*, 11, 1981, pp. 43-59.

476 Ibid, p. 148.

477 Fine, M., and Bowers, C., "Racial identification: The effects of social history and gender." *Journal of Applied Social Psychology*, 14, 1984, pp. 136-146.

478 MacDonald, T. K., and Zannas, M. P., "Cross-dimension ambivalence toward social groups: can ambivalence affect intentions to hire feminists?" *Personality and Social Psychology Bulletin*, 24, 1998, pp. 427-441.

479 Katz, I., *Stigma: A Social Psychological Analysis*, Hillsdale, NJ: Lawrence Erlbaum, 1981.

480 Jost, John T., and Burgess, Diana, "Attitudinal ambivalence and the conflict between group and system justification motives in low status groups," *Personality and Social Psychology Bulletin*, 26, 2000, pp. 293-305.

481 Sidanus. Levin, S., Frederico, C. M., and Pratto, F., "legitimizing ideologies: The social dominance approach," In Jost, J. T., and Major, B., (Eds.), *The Psychology of Legitimacy: Emerging Perspectives on Ideology, Justice and Intergroup Relations*, Cambridge: Cambridge University Press, 2001.

482 Major, B., and Schumaker, T., "legitimacy and the construal of social advantage," in Jost, J. T., and Major, B., (Eds.), Op.cit.

483 Steele, C. M., "Race and the schooling of black Americans," *The Atlantic Monthly*, April 1991, pp. 67-78.

484 Ellemers, N., "Individual upward mobility and the perceived legitimacy of *intergroup* relations," Op. cit.

485 Marmot, M. G., *The Status Syndrome*, NY, NY: Henry Holt, 2004.

486 Marmot, M. G., Rose, G., Shipley, M., and Hamilton, P. I. S., "Employment grade and coronary heart disease in British civil servants," *Journal of Epidemiol Community Health*, 32, 1978, pp. 244-249.

487 Antonovsky, A., "Social class, life expectancy, and overall mortality," *Milbank Memorial Fund Quarterly*, 45, 1967, pp. 31-73.

488 Wray, Linda A., Alwin, Duane F., and McCammon, Ryan J., "Social status and risky health behavior: results from the health and retirement study," *Journal of Gerontology: Social Sciences*, 60: pp. 585-592., 2005.

489 Rablen, Matthew D., and Oswald, Andrew J., "Mortality and Immortality: The Nobel Prize as an experiment into the effect of status on longevity. *Working Paper*, University of Warwick, 24 March 2008.

490 Tiffin, Paul A., and Pearce, mark S., "Social mobility over the lifecourse and self reported mental health at age 50: Prospective cohort study," *Journal of Epidemiology and Community Health*, 59, 2005, pp. 870-872.

491 Adler, N. E., Epel, E. S., Castellazo, G., and Ickovics, J. R., "Relationship of subjective and objective social status with psychological and physiological functioning: preliminary data in healthy, white women," *Health Psychology*, 19, 6, 2000, pp. 586-592.

492 Singh-Manoux, A., Marmot, M. G., and Adler, N. E., "Does subjective social status predict health and change in health status better than objective status? *Psychomatic Medecine*, 67, 6, 2005, pp. 855-861.

493 Dunn, J. R., Veenstra, G., and Ross, N., "Psychosocial and neo-material dimensions of socioeconomic position and health revisited: predictors of self-rated health in a Canadian national survey," *Social Science and Medecine*, 62, 6, 1982, pp. 1465-1473.

494 Cheng, Y. H., Chi, I., Boey, K. W., Ko, L. S. F., and Chou, K. L., "Self-rated economic conditions and healthy of elderly

persons in Hong Kong," *Social science and Medecine*, 55, 8, 2002, pp. 1415-1424.

495 Hu, P., Adler, N., Goldman, N., Weinstein, M., and Seeman, T. E., "Retaliation between subjective social status and measures of health in older Taiwanese persons," *Journal of the American Geriatrics Society*, 53, 3, 2005, pp. 483-498.

496 Reitzel, L. R., Vichina, J. I., Li, Yisheng, Mullen, P. D., Velasquez, M. M., Cinciripini, P. M., Cofta-Woerpel, L., Greisinger, A., and Wetter, D. W., "The influence of subjective social status on vulnerability to postpartum smoking among young pregnant women," *American Journal of Public Health*, 10, 2006.

497 Marmot, M. G., "Status syndrome: A challenge to medicine," *Journal of the American Medical Association*, 11, 295, 2006.

498 Cohen, S., Doyle, W. S., Skoner, D. P., Rabin, B. S., and Gwaltney, J. M., "Social ties and susceptibility to the common cold," *Journal of the American Medical Association*, 277, 1997, pp. 1940-44.

499 Berkman, L. F., and Glass, T., "Social integration, social networks, social support, and health," In Berkman, L. F., and Kawachi, I., (Eds.), *Social Epidemiology*, NY, NY: Oxford university press, 2000, pp. 137-173.

500 Hemingway, H., Shipley, M., Brunner, E., Britton, A., Malik, M., and Marmot, M. G., "Does autonomic function link social position to coronary risk? The Whitehall II Study," *Circulation*, 111, 2005, pp. 3071-3077.

501 Cherkas, L. F., Aviv, A., Valdes, A. M., Hunkin, J. L., Gardner, J. P., Surdulescu, G. L., Kimura, M., and Spector, T. D., "The effects of social status on biological aging as measured by white-blood-cell telomere length," *Aging Cell*, 5, 5, 2006, pp. 361-365.

502 Kerbo, Harold, *Social Stratification and Inequality: Class Conflict in the United States*, NY: McGraw-Hill Book Co., 1983, p. 113.

503 Kriesberg, Louis, *Constructive Conflicts: from Escalation to Resolution*, 2nd Edition, Oxford: Rowman and Littlefield Publishers, 2003, p. 15.
504 Maiese, Michelle, "Social status," in *Beyond Intractability*, Eds. Burgess, grey, and Burguess, Heidi. Conflict Research Consortium, University of Colorado, Boulder, Poste: September 2004.
505 Lenski, G. E., "Status crystallization: A non-vertical dimension of status," *American Sociological Review*, 19, 1954, pp. 405-413.
506 Lenski, G. E., "Social participation and status crystallization," *American Sociological Review*, 21, 1956, pp. 458-64.
507 Geschwender, J., "Continuities in the study of status consistency and cognitive dissonance," *Social Forces*, 46, 1967, pp. 160-171.
508 Ibid.
509 Davis, K., and Moore, W.E., "Some principles of stratification," *American Sociological Review*, Vol 10, 1945, pp. 242-9.
510 Frank, R. H., *Choosing the Right Pond: Human Behavior and the Quest from relative Wage*, Oxford: Oxford University press, London, 1985.
511 Weber, M., *Economy and Society*, Berkeley: University of California press, 1978.
512 Galizzi, M., and lang, K., "Relative wages, wage growth, and quit behavior," *Journal of Labor Economics*, 16, 1998, pp. 367-391.
513 Kelman, H. C., "Process of opinion change," *Public Opinion Quarterly*, 25, 1961, pp. 57-78.
514 Weiss. Yoram, and Fershtman, Chaim, "Social status and economic performance: A survey," *European Economic Review*, 42, 1998, p. 802.
515 Ibid, p. 803.
516 Cialdini, Robert B., "Indirect tactics of image management: Beyond basking," In Giacalone, R. A., and Rosenfeld, P. (Eds.), *Impression Management in the Organizations*, Hinsdale, NH: Erlbaum, 1989, pp. 45-56.

517 Lynn, Freda B., and Podolny, Joel M., "A sociological (de)construction of the relationship between status and quality," *Harvard University*, March 10, 2005.

518 Ridgeway, Cecilia L., "Status in groups: The importance of motivation," *American Sociological Review*, 47, 1982, pp. 76-88.

519 Turner, J., "Social categorization and social discrimination in the minimal group paradigm," In Tajfel, H., (Ed.), *Differentiation between Social Groups: Studies in the Social psychology of Intergroup Relations*, London, UK: Academic Press, Inc, 1978.

520 Turner, J. C., and brown, R. J., "Status, position and legitimacy in inter-group behavior: The effects of different status relationships on in-group bias and group creativity," *In Tajfel, H., Op.cit.*

521 Cummins, B., and Lockwood, J., "The effects of status differences, favored treatment and equity on inter-group comparisons," *European Journal of Social Psychology*, 9, 1979, pp. 281-289.

522 Sachdev, I., and Bourkis, R. Y., "Status differentials and intergroup behavior," *European Journal of Social Psychology*, 17, 1987, pp. 277-293.

523 Benoit-Smullyan, Emile, "Status, status types, and status interrelations," *American Sociological Review*, 9, 1944, p.151.

524 Archibald. W. P., "Face-to-face: the alienating effects of class, status and power divisions," *American Sociological Review*, 41, 1970, pp. 819-837.

525 Long, Jack M., Lynch, James J., Machiran, N. M., Thomas, Sue A., and Manilow, Kenneth, "The effects of status on blood pressure during verbal communication," *Journal of Behavioral Medecine*, 5, 2, 1982, pp. 165-71.

526 Milner, Murray, *Status and sacredness: A general theory of status relations and an analysis of Indian culture*. New York" Oxford University press, 1994.

527 Lerner, M. J., "The desire for justice and reactions to victims," In Macaulay, J., and Berkowitz, L., (Eds.), *Altruism and Helping Behavior*, NY: Academic Press, 1970.

528 Hagendoorn, L., and Henke, R., "The effects of multiple category membership on intergroup evaluation in a north Indian context: Class, caste, and religion," *British Journal of Psychology*, 30, 1991, pp. 247-260.

529 Torrance, E. Paul, "Some consequences of power differences on decision making in permanent and temporary three-man groups," In hare, A. P., Borgotta, E. F., and Bales, R. F., (Eds.), *Small Groups*, NY: Knopf, 1955.

530 Willis, Alex, "On the tip of creative tongues,: *The New York Times* , October 4, 2009.

531 Useem. Michael, and Karabel, Jerome, "Pathways to top corporate management," *American Sociological Review*, 51, 1986, pp. 184-200.

532 Lin, Nan, Ensel, Walter M., and Vaughan, John C., "Social resources and occupational status attainment," *Social Forces*, 59, 1981, pp. 1-40.

533 Belliveau, Mara A., O'Reilly III, Charles A., and Wade, James B., "Social capital at the top: Effects of social similarity and status on CEO compensation," *Academy of Management Journal*, 39, 1996, pp. 1568-1593.

534 Blinder, A., "The challenge of high unemployment," *American Economic Review*, 78, 2, 1988, pp. 1-15.

535 Frank, R., "Are workers paid their marginal products?" *American Economic Review*, 74, 1984, pp. 549-70.

536 Fershtman, Chaim, and Weiss, Yoram, "Social rewards, externalities and stable preferences," *Journal of Public Economics*, 70, 1998, pp. 55-73.

537 Ibid, p. 53.

538 Weiss, Yoram, and Fershtman, Chaim, Op. cit, p. 803.

539 Bate, S., "Women on the verge of a serious shakedown," *Marketing Week*, 15, 1993, pp. 37-40.

540 Underwood, E., "Luxury's tide turns," *Brandweek*, 35, 1994, pp. 18-22.

541 Ball, Sheryl, Eckel, Catherine, Grossman, Philip J., and Zane, William," Status in markets," *The Quarterly Journal of Economics*, February 2001, pp. 161-188.

542 Ibid, pp. 187-88.

543 Ball, Sheryl B., and Eckel, Catherine C., "Stars upon thars: Status and discrimination in ultimum games," *Unpublished Manuscript*

544 Ball. Sheryl B., and Eckel, Catherine C., "Buying status: Experimental evidence on status in negotiations," *Psychology and Marketing*, 13, 4, 1996, pp. 381-405.

545 Thomas, Dana, *How Luxury Lost Its Luster*, Penguin Books, NY, 2007.

546 Robson, Arthur J., "Status, the distribution of wealth, private and social attitudes to risk," *Econometrica*, LX, 1992, pp. 837-857.

547 Ng, Yew-Kwang, and Wang, Jianguo," Relative income, aspiration, environmental quality, individual and political myopia," *Mathematical Social Sciences*, XXVI. 1993, pp. 2-23.

548 Fershtman, Chaim, and Weiss, Yoram, "Social status, culture and economic performance," *Economic Journal*, CIII, 1993, pp. 946-959.

549 Congleton, Roger D., "Efficient status seeking: Externalities and the evolution of status games," *Journal of Economic behavior and Organizations*, XI, 1989, pp. 175-190.

Made in the USA
Middletown, DE
26 May 2020

95853117R00146